Split

True Stories of Relationship Breakdown in Ireland

Rachel Fehily

This edition published in 2011 by
Y Books
Lucan, Co. Dublin, Ireland
Tel/fax: +353 1 6217992
publishing@ybooks.ie
www.ybooks.ie

Paperback ISBN: 978-1-908023-30-8
Ebook – Mobi format ISBN: 978-1-908023-31-5
Ebook – epub format ISBN: 978-1-908023-32-2

A CIP catalogue record for this book is available from the British Library.
10 9 8 7 6 5 4 3 2 1

Typeset by Y Books
Cover design by Graham Thew Design
Author photo by Simon Martin
Cover images: www.stockphoto.com
Printed and bound by CPI Group (UK) Ltd, Croydon, CR0 4YY

contents

disclaimer

Names, dates, locations, occupations and other distinguishing details have been changed to protect the identities of the contributors, their families and any other person referred to in the stories. All the stories are based on the personal experiences, opinions and emotions of the contributors and do not purport to be absolute statements of fact about any other person.

acknowledgements

Thank you to all the anonymous contributors who generously gave their time and shared their stories so that others could learn from their experiences.

I would also like to thank all the following people for their friendship, help and encouragement:

Richard Bennett, Judy Blake, Rhona Boylan, Patricia Bunyan, Lana Citron, Aidan Cosgrave, Juliet Cronin, Rachel Dalton, John Diamond, Emily Egan, Eric Fehily, Natalie Dion-Fehily, Sarah Fehily, Ben and Jennifer Fehily, Jane and Christian Fehily, Morgan Fehily, Max and Anne Fehily, Eleanor Flegg, Alexander Gibbs, Eugene Gleeson, Jennifer Gordon, David and Pam Harris, Sue and Charlie Harvey, Victoria Larson Kavanagh, Mary Kelly, Conor Mackey, Mimi McArdle, John McKeon, Stephen Mulvey, John Murphy, Helene O'Brien, Catherine O'Grady, John O'Grady and his family, Aisling O'Kelly, Carla O'Kelly, Mark O'Mahony, Pat O'Mahony, Avril O'Riordan, Luigi Rea, Aideen Ryan, Martin Thomas, Iseult White, Kieron Wood.

And thank you to Robert Doran and Chenile Keogh at Y Books for their invaluable input into every aspect of this book.

introduction

People stay in bad relationships for too long for many different reasons. Maybe it's because they're afraid to be on their own or because they don't want to upset their children. It can be that they feel they have no choice because if they leave they will have nowhere to live or their family will suffer financially. For others it is the fear of the process of breaking up itself that stops them from leaving a loveless, dysfunctional or abusive relationship. And, of course, many aren't given a choice – it is their partners who choose to leave the relationship and they are forced to rebuild a life that they had never planned for.

I wrote *Split* because I think it helps in this situation to hear stories that are similar to your own. Stories help us to put our own situation into context. As humans we relate on a very deep level to the experiences of others. If we can follow another person's emotional journey and identify with it, we can learn more about ourselves, and it can help us to find solutions to our own problems. Also, relationship breakdown is something that happens behind closed doors, in private, so it's only possible to hear stories when other people are willing to share them.

All the contributors to this book experienced the trauma of relationship breakdown and came out the other side, and they have been generous enough to share their stories with me so that others might benefit from their experience. Their stories provide constructive advice, comfort and inspiration for others who are dealing with a break-up.

The book is also written for anyone who has a professional or personal interest in the effects of relationship breakdown. If you're a therapist or a family lawyer, the stories will give you a broader insight into the experience of your client. Likewise, if you have a friend or family member going through a break-up, this book will help you to understand their situation and support them.

In compiling the book, I asked friends, family and acquaintances if they knew people who had been through a relationship breakdown and if they would be willing to talk to me. Surprisingly, I didn't have any problem finding people who were willing to be involved. I was very impressed by how articulate the contributors were and by how open they were about their stories. They participated on the understanding that their identities would be protected and I know they had an understanding of how valuable their stories could be to others. They are all Irish and they all live in Ireland. Names, occupations, locations and certain details have been changed to protect their identities, but the essence, emotions and experiences described in their stories are all true.

I interviewed people who had been through the process of separation or divorce and had come out the other side, rather than approaching people who were in the middle of the process and perhaps couldn't see the wood for the trees. I felt it was important that each story was complete.

I deliberately tried to interview the same number of

men as women. There are some differences in the way the sexes express themselves but I think the stories expose more similarities than differences in the way both men and women experience separation.

What is strikingly clear from the stories is that the breakdown of a relationship is as devastating as bereavement, and many of the contributors described it in that way. If someone you love dies, there's nothing you can do about it. You go through the grieving process and it's final. If your relationship ends, your ex is still alive and possibly with someone else. You may still have to communicate with them because you have children together and outstanding legal and financial issues. This process is incredibly difficult for most people and impossible for some.

Rejection and abandonment are heartbreaking for adults and children. The person you loved and shared your life with still exists but is no longer there for you. You are often left with problems to solve after the break up around parenting responsibilities, money and property. Parenting apart is a huge challenge; both parties usually suffer financially when they each have to set up a household after a break up. The contributors looked for help from lawyers, health care professionals, mediators and friends. It's interesting to examine the type of help they received – the quality varies enormously.

Conflict around parenting apart can be extremely difficult to resolve. It helps enormously if both parents support each other, co-operate and try to keep conflict to a minimum. I strongly believe that parents have to put their children first if their relationship ends. It's not right to use children as pawns or to expect them to take sides or be inappropriately involved in arguments or discussions. For example, it's incredibly damaging to use the fact that you are arguing about finances with your ex as a good reason to withhold access to your child. A break-up is an adult problem that adults must work out between themselves. After a break-up both parents should continue to support each other as parents unless a child is being abused or is truly in danger with the other parent. I think the stories illustrate that the best thing you can do when you are finding parenting apart difficult is to keep looking for professional help and to find people whose advice you can trust.

Practicing as a barrister and a mediator has given me a very broad experience of conflict resolution. I have often felt sympathy for people who ended up in court – it isn't always helpful or necessary. I have found that in some situations the adversarial legal process can be damaging to litigants both emotionally and financially. More people are being encouraged by the government to mediate in family law cases, but I think there is a need for the process of mediation to be properly structured and incorporated into the family law system.

Mediation should always be supported by legal advice and separating couples shouldn't be forced to sit in a room together while they are negotiating. In my experience mediation for separating couples often works better if I see both parties separately and make sure that they get independent legal advice about financial matters and professional advice on parenting issues, if necessary.

As a mediator I give very practical advice and help people who are separating to identify and narrow down the issues that they disagree on. If both parties have an intermediary they can trust, then the process of separation can be faster, easier and less expensive. Not every conflict has to end with a winner and a loser. Often people simply need to be heard, learn to improve their communication skills or get solid advice from experienced and well-qualified professionals so that they can resolve their conflict and move forward.

Every time a relationship ends the situation has the potential to turn into a small but costly war. The damage can be physical, emotional and financial. If a break-up is inevitable then you must try to make it as amicable as possible, for your own sake and the sake of everyone around you. It's not easy and sometimes it's impossible. If it is impossible then you ought to seek legal advice. But you should try mediation, negotiation and everything else available to you before you get to the door of a courtroom.

If you have to go to war, arm yourself with the best knowledge and legal advice possible. Take your time, get support and make sure you're strong and prepared for the long haul.

There are lots of government and non-governmental agencies that dedicate themselves to supporting couples and families. Make sure you do your research and make yourself aware of all the options that are open to you. The most important advice I can give to you is that you should try to minimise conflict in your life and look after yourself and the people you love. These stories show that human beings are incredibly loving, resilient and optimistic. So no matter how difficult your break up was, don't let it define you. When it's over it's time to move on. Don't live in the past and allow yourself to be consumed by your relationship breakdown or you will miss out on the wonderful opportunities in your future.

❋ ❋ ❋

'When we meet real tragedy in life, we can react in two ways – either by losing hope or falling into self-destructive habits, or by using the challenge to find our inner strength.'

Dalai Lama XIV

gerry

out of the darkness

Gerry[*] is a lovely gentle giant. He met his wife Janet when he came to work as a garda in Dublin. She was a chronic alcoholic and made life miserable for him and their children throughout their marriage.

When Gerry decided that he'd had enough and tried to get a separation, all hell broke loose. Janet accused him of assaulting her and of sexually abusing their children. The children were taken into foster care and Gerry worked with the system until he got them back.

Janet's life became more difficult as she descended to rock bottom. Gerry tried hard to protect his children and has now rebuilt their lives together.

I'm originally from the West of Ireland and am the eldest of seven children. I was brought up on a small farm with a dairy and some cattle. We were so innocent about life back then. I went to the local school where I got a good education but I didn't know anything of the outside world. During the summer I would work for the neighbouring farmers. They were happy times.

When I finished school I did a business course in Galway for two years. After I finished that I applied to join the gardaí, and in 1977 I was called up to go to train in Templemore.

---

[*] Names, occupations, locations and other identifying details have been altered to protect identities

There was a change of government in 1977, with Fianna Fáil replacing the Fine Gael/Labour coalition. The government sent nearly every new recruit up to Dublin because their policy was to put more gardaí on the streets, so it was a good time to apply. We had to be at least 5 ft 8" tall and there was a mandatory chest measurement as well. I remember taking a deep breath before I was measured and I barely made it.

Templemore was very rigid in those days. There was no getting out at weekends; it was all about the training. We didn't get to see our families for months. I was nineteen and it was my first time away from home. It was a big change, putting all my things in a suitcase and heading off on my own.

After six months of training we were expected to know a lot. We learned about family law, road traffic law, accidents, murders, suicides, fisheries and wildlife. I remember learning about all kinds of things that seemed irrelevant at the time, like how to recognise noxious weeds and birds' nests. The training was very broad because after only six months you'd have the power of arrest and there'd be no one there to tell you what to do.

I came to Dublin to work as a guard in 1978. They sent nearly everyone up to Dublin because there was a fair bit of social unrest at the time and they needed more guards.

I lived in a Garda station for my first two years in Dublin. That was handy for work but not great for my social life. The accommodation was very basic and we didn't have any proper facilities. I shared a room with six other guys and there was always a dreadful smell of socks and sweat.

I had been living in Dublin for about a year when I met

Janet in a nightclub. Janet was very petite and very attractive and we were attracted to each other immediately. We came from very different backgrounds. She was from inner-city Dublin and her father had left the family when she was small and her mother had gone to work as a cleaner and brought up the three children alone. Janet didn't get a good education. Instead of going to secondary school she had to go out and work. She didn't even get to sit her Inter Cert.

We socialised with other guards and friends and we used to go to dances and pubs after we had finished our shifts. I would work seven nights in a row and then I'd get Monday and Tuesday nights off. Sometimes I'd get mid-week breaks and the odd time I'd get a long weekend. Each tour of duty was eight hours. Janet worked in a gentleman's club, so her hours were all over the place as well, and we often ended up drinking together very late at night.

Things started out OK. We did all the usual things that couples do when they're going out together – spending time together, going to dances and pubs, just having fun. I met her mother in Dublin, and after a few months I brought her home to meet my parents.

I soon noticed that Janet was very controlling. She had to be the boss about where we went, what time we went there and who we socialised with. She was very particular about my clothes and was always telling me what to wear. She wouldn't ever let me wear jeans, for example.

I also noticed that Janet drank a lot. She could hold a certain amount, but after a while she would become even more controlling than usual. If she wanted to be somewhere, we couldn't leave and if she wanted to go somewhere else, we had to go immediately – everything was her way or no way.

There is an old adage that says 'love is blind'. My parents were a bit uneasy with Janet when they met her and others could see that she had a lot of control over me. I thought it was the way things were in a relationship. I didn't have a lot of experience with women, so I accepted it. I thought all this was normal.

We got married two years after we met, in a hotel in Dublin. I was having palpitations all the time leading up to the wedding because I was afraid Janet would get drunk and throw one of her tantrums. Whenever she got angry she'd always blame me. She'd say, 'Look at him; he's after not being on time,' or I'd be wearing the wrong clothes or something. There was a lot of verbal abuse. When I was on my own with her it would get physical too.

She used to tease me and taunt me and tell me to hit her when she was drunk and angry. She'd say, 'Just because you're in the job you're in you think you can get away with it.' Whenever she was like that I would always turn and walk away. She'd say 'Look at you; you're only a coward.'

I don't know why Janet was like that. Maybe her mother gave her a hard time, but it doesn't seem likely because they always had a close relationship. Perhaps it was her father who was violent, but he was never talked about and he was only around until she was five or six, so I don't know. I always walked away from her when she tried to provoke me. I was never going to hit a woman. I was the same as I was on the playing field or as a guard – I would never resort to violence.

I remember going to a dance when I was young, and some drunk guy came up to me and head-butted me in the face for no reason. I was totally shocked but I just walked away. I never retaliated because that's the kind of person I am.

When I met Janet first she was drinking shorts but after a few years she began drinking wine. She could drink one, two or more bottles of wine a day. She used to hit me in the back when she was drunk and I'd run away from her. Later, after we were married, I'd be afraid to go to sleep in case she'd attack me. I became a light sleeper and I was always aware if she was moving around the house. I'd hear a certain type of footstep and I'd know she was going to attack me. More often than not I'd go into the bathroom and lock myself in there just, to get away from her.

We decided after we married to live outside Dublin on a small farm. I kept a few animals on the field. About five years into the marriage Janet gave up working in the club to become a full-time housewife. I didn't mind, but we had no kids and she only had to look after the two of us, so there wasn't a huge amount of housework. She used to go into town and meet up with her mother and shop, but she stopped seeing her friends so much and became quite isolated, drinking alone in the house a lot.

I suggested Alcoholics Anonymous to her many, many times but she always insisted that she didn't have a problem. There was no way to convince her.

I reached the end of my tether about six or seven years into the marriage. We didn't have kids and Janet was drinking all the time. She was provoking me, abusing me and threatening me constantly. She had injured me a few times. I remember I collected her one time and she wanted to go into a pub. I was driving the car and I refused to stop. She took off her stiletto shoe and hit me in the back of the head. I was lucky I didn't crash. I had to go into work the next day with a hole in my head.

Incidents like that happened quite often and, looking back, it's amazing that I stayed with her. I suppose I felt responsible for her and I thought I could cure her alcoholism, and I didn't want to leave my home and give up on my marriage.

My main source of support at that time was Al-Anon, the support group for friends and family of alcoholics who are affected by alcoholics or are finding it hard to live with alcoholics. I was on the programme to help me deal with the effects of living with Janet and it gave me great help with coping with it all. They said I should stick it out and only make decisions for myself. Al-Anon was passive but it did help keep me sane. I loved the Serenity Prayer: 'God, grant me the serenity to accept the things I cannot change, the courage to change the things I can, and the wisdom to know the difference.'

What the prayer told me was that I had to look after myself and she had to look after herself. I also found the 'three C's' helpful: 'I didn't cause her disease, I can't cure it and I can't control it.'

I had support from my family too. However, I was gradually losing contact with my friends, family and work colleagues. I didn't want to go to parties, weddings or any other social occasions because I was scared about what Janet might do if we went out together. I didn't want to go to things on my own because I would have felt out of it. Everyone went to these events as couples and I'd have to explain why Janet wasn't there. I was sick of making excuses for her.

Fifteen years into our marriage Janet decided she wanted to have children. There was no planning it together – she decided and that was that. She was thirty-eight at the time and I was forty. We had three beautiful children fairly close together. Janet was a good mother in the beginning. She looked after the children and did all the cooking and cleaning. I did my share too, and I used to get up in the middle of the night to feed them.

Janet drank throughout her pregnancies and she smoked over thirty cigarettes a day. I don't know how she had the stamina to do the drinking she did – she was at most seven stone. It used to worry me a lot. I remember when she was in hospital after having the babies, all the nurses and doctors advised her not to smoke but of course she didn't listen to them. It's amazing that the kids are so well. They're perfectly fine as regards intelligence, and physically they are very well. They are so bright and there is no sign of foetal alcohol syndrome or anything like that.

After a while communication and cooperation broke down completely and Janet was drinking very heavily. She'd take the children off into town and I wouldn't know where they had gone. She'd often be with her mother, sitting in her flat drinking and talking. God knows what the kids were doing. The children were never left alone when they were babies; I just about managed to fill in the gaps when she wasn't there.

At the time I was doing very well with the gardaí and I used to go to a lot of conferences. I brought her to one or two but she made a total show of herself and me. I said to myself: 'What am I doing? Why am I bringing her?' and I stopped asking her to come along.

One time we were at a conference together in Galway. We'd left the children with my mother, who lived nearby. While we were there my father got very sick and had to go to hospital. The next day he got worse – he'd had an aneurism and when they scoped him to see it, it bled badly and he was taken into intensive care.

While all this was happening Janet was very bad. We took the children back to Dublin and I said to her: 'I need to go and see my father and my mother; he's very sick.' She had a fit and said, 'You're going nowhere.' She put the baby in my arms and drove off in a drunken state. I couldn't understand why she wouldn't let me go. I was always around when she wanted me. I didn't play golf all day or go to the pub. I took care of everything for her. I often had to ring in sick and take care of the kids when she was off drinking.

So I was left with the kids for the evening until she came back. As soon as she went to bed and I knew she was asleep, I sneaked out of the house so I could drive to Galway to see my father. I had been in touch with my sister and I knew they were going to switch off his life-support machine. On the way down to Galway I got a phone call saying that he had passed away. I never got a chance to say goodbye to my father.

When I got back to the house that morning, Janet said: 'Where the hell were you?' and she accused me of being with someone else. I said that I had been trying to see my dying father and that he had passed away. I told her that I had to go to the funeral and help my family to make all the arrangements. She wouldn't go to the funeral with me, so I had to go on my own.

I remember the day of the funeral; I was very upset and I was worried about leaving the kids alone with Janet. I had to do a reading and carry my father's coffin. I called her after the burial and she said: 'You'd better get home; I've no food for the kids.' I left my mother and my family and said that I had to get back home because Janet was sick. I'm sure they all knew what was going on. I was fed up telling lies to cover up for her.

Somehow or other I managed to get on with my job. I was an ordinary guard but I was very ambitious. I moved up the ranks and became a sergeant and then an inspector. I found the work very interesting and I loved being able to help people.

In 2002 I applied to work for the United Nations Peacekeeping Force. I was given a post to go and serve in Cyprus for a year. I was delighted because I wanted to go out there and help with conflict resolution. It was something I had incorporated into my work and my personal life – always trying to help reduce conflict wherever I went. Janet created a huge amount of conflict. She was so argumentative about every detail of our lives. I always had to do things her way. We discussed going to Cyprus at length. There was obviously a lot of preparation involved. We had to rent out our family home in Ireland, rent a place in Cyprus, get injections and organise schools for the kids. It was going to be expensive to go there but I thought it would be a great opportunity for us all as a family.

I hoped that things would change while we were abroad. I thought it would be good for us both to get away from Dublin and maybe in a new setting we'd get on better. Janet depended a lot on her mother and her mother would always take her side if we were arguing. Her mother saw no wrong in anything Janet did and no matter what happened she was in the right and I was in the wrong.

Janet made lots of unrealistic promises while we were planning to go away. She said that when we were in Cyprus drink wouldn't be an issue. In Ireland she felt alone and isolated where we lived. In Cyprus we were going to live in a community in the city so it would be totally different.

The Irish gardaí out in Cyprus all stuck together so it was like an extension of being in Ireland. There were twenty other guards out there with their wives and children, so it should have been great fun, having such a big gang of friends. Instead it was a nightmare.

My hours were fantastic. I worked from 7.30 a.m. every morning until 3.30 p.m. in the afternoon. That meant I could spend lots of time with the children. I would take them to the beach, the pool or go out travelling for the day on trips to Limassol or Ayia Napa. In the beginning I asked Janet to come with us but she never wanted to go, so I eventually stopped asking her. I'd take the kids out on my own and every evening when we came back she'd be drunk.

The other wives used to wonder where Janet was, so I'd say: 'She's at home,' or 'She's not feeling well,' or 'She doesn't mix well.' On one occasion the other wives invited Janet for a night out and it was a total disaster. She got drunk and abused everyone in her company. I think the trip to Cyprus was the final straw for our relationship. It finished our home, our kids, everything.

Things were deteriorating and her symptoms were getting worse. She drank a huge amount of wine while we were away because it was very cheap. She was going downhill and she had some really bad episodes in Cyprus. She would buy lots of beer and cases of wine and sit at home and drink it all.

I tried so hard to get doctors to talk to Janet. I met this fantastic doctor in Cyprus, who tried her utmost to get her to stop drinking. She went over to see her on some pretext or other, but as soon as she brought up the topic of her drinking, Janet walked out on her. No one could get through to her.

During all of this the kids were living in fear. Janet was very loud and aggressive when she was drunk and she didn't care who heard her or who was affected by her behaviour. She never cared how late she stayed out and she often kept the kids with her wherever she was. She'd be out in a bar or a restaurant and she'd have the children with her. I'm sure the kids have terrible memories of that time.

After Cyprus I decided that I'd had enough. I wanted to get a separation. I'd given everything I could to the relationship and I had no more to give. I realised I had to protect myself and the kids.

That is when the trouble really started. We were basically living in separate rooms and whenever I engaged with her Janet was abusive and violent. She was aggressive towards the kids, shouting at them and intimidating them. They weren't being looked after properly. They weren't being fed, educated or clothed properly.

I went to a solicitor around 2004 so that I could initiate separation proceedings. At that stage we were still living together so I applied for a protection order. This was so that Janet couldn't be threatening, violent or abusive towards me or the children while we were living together. As soon as I got the order against her she made an application for me to be barred from the house. Being a guard this was totally humiliating and embarrassing for me. There were a few hearings in the District Court in Dolphin House about our protection order and barring order and then it all went to the Circuit Court because I had issued separation proceedings.

I agreed to leave the house voluntarily so there was no need for a barring order in the end. I went to live in a friend's cottage that was near to where we lived. It needed to be renovated, so I did it up in lieu of rent.

Janet had a legal aid solicitor, so our solicitors were talking to each other and negotiating on our behalf. My children were very young at the time – eight, six and four. I was allowed access on Wednesdays in the cottage and I saw them on alternate Saturdays as well. I didn't have bedrooms for them at the cottage, so they couldn't stay overnight with me.

This arrangement didn't last long. When I was dropping the kids back, Janet wouldn't let me past the front gate of the house and she made me hand them back to her over the gate. The kids didn't like that and they'd get upset when I brought them home. They said they didn't want to go back to her. They used to say to me, 'Will you ring Mammy and tell her I want to stay with you?' They were worried about me and they'd say, 'Will you not be lonely on your own? We'll stay with you Daddy.'

They were going back to a woman who was sitting in a back room on her own and drinking and smoking all day. They used to say, 'That's Mammy's room in there,' and they didn't want to disturb her.

I was only a few miles away and I'd drive by and look at

the house. I was broken-hearted leaving them. I knew they were missing school. Janet would take them into town to see her mother in her little Corporation flat and stay there all day with them. The kids would sit around doing nothing.

Janet wouldn't agree to anything to do with the separation. She was very obstructive. After I had paid the mortgage and her maintenance, I didn't have a penny left for myself.

The kids started to miss too many days of school and were very tired when they were in school. That's when I called the social workers and they got involved. They had the children under the supervision of the Health Board and the District Court made a Section 47 enquiry order, which meant that the Children's Services had to carry out an investigation to see if they should take any action to protect the children. Janet went to the gardaí around this time and told them that I had assaulted her and sexually abused the children. She had no evidence of this. I think she was becoming mentally unbalanced and had convinced herself that I'd attacked her. She needed to justify her own behaviour and she could only do this by making me out to be in the wrong.

What really happened was that she had been trying to attack me while I was locked in a room. She was banging on the door with a hammer. I couldn't get out the window of the room because it was too small, so I had to get out the door. I opened it a little and she put her hand in to grab my hair. I passed by her and pushed her out of the way and she said that this was an assault on her. I had taken photographs of the hammer marks on the door and the gardaí saw these and believed my statement. A file was sent to the DPP but they decided not to prosecute me. I didn't get any advantage for being a garda. I was treated fairly, but my colleagues were horrified by all this.

Then Janet went off to Women's Aid with the children. I had no idea where they were. I actually reported her missing. I was very worried because there was a news report on television that a woman in Wexford had walked into the sea with her two children. I firmly believed it was Janet and two of my children. I was terrified until I found out it wasn't them.

When I suspected that they were in the shelter I went to see if they were there and stood outside and looked in. I stood on a pillar and in the distance I could see the children playing in the garden. After the ordeal of thinking that they might be dead, I was dying to see them. I stood there with a friend, crying and upset. My friend said to me, 'C'mon we'll get them; we'll go in and take them.' I said, 'No, I'll go the courts route.' It's amazing how people think that that's a good way to go about things.

Janet stayed in Women's Aid for three or four weeks and they supported her and helped her to go to the gardaí so she could make her allegations. I suppose they had to go on her word until all the investigations were carried out.

While all this was happening I felt the courts weren't really listening to what I had to say. I wasn't given an opportunity to talk. When Janet took the children away to Women's Aid and accused me of physically assaulting her and sexually abusing the children, everything had to be investigated. Once she made these allegations I was only allowed to see the children under supervision. I had to see them in a health centre while the gardaí, social workers and the courts were all making their inquiries. Janet was making up really far-fetched stories. I think she was trying to convince herself that something had happened. The kids were very young and very vulnerable. The gardaí questioned the kids and decided that the situation didn't warrant bringing them to the Rape Crisis Centre.

When we were in court Janet would come in with black sunglasses on and she looked very unwell. I know that some of the judges thought that there was something wrong with her. It took some time but eventually the social workers started to see that there was something amiss when she failed to keep appointments with them. When they called to the house to see her, they saw that she was drinking, not getting out of bed and not taking the kids to school.

During the time all this madness was going on and the social workers were carrying out their investigations, I told them the whole story and said that I was applying for sole custody of the children.

The court ordered an assessment of the situation by a child psychologist. He was brilliant. He made appointments to see Janet and spoke with all the family. He immediately grasped the fact that she couldn't parent and was mentally unstable and an alcoholic. While all this was going on the children were taken into care with a foster family.

It took a long time for everything to get sorted out. The children were in foster care for ten weeks over the summer and Janet went to live in town. I remember the day in 2005 when I finally got custody of the children. I had to show the social workers my plan to care for them and I had to get a minder for them.

The Judge gave me a very fair hearing. I wanted him to cancel the care order, give me sole custody of the children and bar Janet from the house. He granted all the orders and Janet was barred from the house. I'll never forget going directly from the courthouse over to where the children were staying to bring them home. When I got to the house where they were staying in foster care they were all dressed, packed and ready to go. I felt like I was on top of the world coming back home with them all.

I had persevered for months and months because I wanted to do things right. I understood how the system worked because I was a guard. I knew that no judge would make any final order without evidence or proof from an independent, competent person. I knew that no matter what I said or Janet said, the judge would have to rely on independent evidence.

❋ ❋ ❋

Men don't talk and men don't cry. Women can go out and talk to each other, they can go to Women's Aid and women's refuges, but there is nothing like that for men. That's the reason that men don't do themselves any favours. They turn and walk away because they think it's simpler to do that rather than fight for their children, their marriage and their home. A lot of men give up because they lose their tempers. They think the system is anti-men and weighted against them.

Men hate the feeling that they are just there to provide the money. When it comes to access to their children, they have huge difficulties when it's denied to them. It's the most hurtful thing of all to a man, not to be allowed to see his children. A vindictive, destructive mother can cause parental alienation and stop a father seeing his children for years.

I know lots of people have problems with the family

courts but part of the problem is that they don't cooperate with the system and they are impatient. It took time for me to get to the stage where there was an independent report from a psychologist. Janet didn't keep her appointments and I did. I went to all the appointments and waited until the courts, psychologist, gardaí and social workers did their investigations.

I still had to pay Janet maintenance into her bank account every week, and after she left I had to chase after her to get the children's allowance back. It was very difficult to organise access for her to see the children because she was barred from the house. Some of the neighbours were very helpful and they allowed her to see the children in their homes. That didn't work out because she abused them and their hospitality.

She used the money I gave her to drink and she ended up homeless and living rough or in hostels in the city centre. I lost contact with her for about two years and was always waiting for a phone call to say she'd been found dead. The kids got very worried about her and would ask me where she was. I managed to trace her and I found out that she had actually met someone and moved into a flat with him in the same area where she'd grown up.

She met her boyfriend in a pub. He was fond of drink as well. I think she manipulated him and convinced him that she'd had a hard time with me. While she was living with him I tried to accommodate her access to the children. We used to meet up in hotels or they'd go to Janet's studio apartment for a few hours. At one stage she applied for overnight access but she didn't get it. The children accepted that we couldn't ever live together and they went for a little bit of counselling. I'm sure they were affected by all the things that had happened.

Janet eventually got cancer. That was a horrible time. I knew she had gone for tests because I was still paying for all her medical expenses in private hospitals. I asked her doctor what the prognosis was and he said she had three months. She had ovarian and stomach cancer. I got her into the hospice and I brought the kids to see her when she was unwell. She was in a terribly emaciated state. They gave her massive doses of morphine. It was all horribly stressful. She stayed with her boyfriend until she died. She was fifty when she passed away and he was forty.

I talked to her boyfriend after she died and he told me that she had controlled him and shouted at him a lot. He also told me that when his father had died, she didn't let him go to the funeral: the same kind of thing that had happened to me.

In the final settlement for our divorce I got the house and I was supposed to sell some of the land attached to it for her settlement. The land was put up for sale but no one was interested in it and she wasn't anxious for me to sell it. I had paid over a lump sum to her from my pension as part of the settlement as well. I discovered after she died that it was still in the bank and now I'm trying to get that back for the kids.

I took time off when all this was going on and then returned to work with the gardaí when everything was sorted out. I had good prospects but I really wanted to look after the children so I retired early. It was the best decision I ever made. I think it is very important for children to have a parent there with them all the time.

I'm in a new relationship now with a lovely woman. She has two children and we're about to take all our kids on holiday together for the first time. I'm really looking forward to it and I have great hopes for the future.

* * *

Al-Anon

In the late 1930s in the United States, close relatives of recovering alcoholics realised that they needed help too. They formed themselves into groups and the groups drew together to become Al-Anon.

The purpose of Al-Anon is to help families and friends of alcoholics recover from the effects of living with the problem drinking of a relative or friend in an anonymous environment. The only requirement for membership is that there be a problem of alcoholism in a relative or friend.

In group meetings the members learn to cope with their problems by sharing their experience, strength and hope.

The Al-Anon twelve-step programme of recovery is adapted from Alcoholics Anonymous and is based upon the Twelve Steps, Twelve Traditions and Twelve Concepts of Service. It is not affiliated with any other organisation or outside entity.

Alateen is part of the Al-Anon fellowship and is for young people aged twelve to seventeen, who are affected by a problem drinker. The members share their ideas and learn to accept it as an illness and to lessen its impact on their lives. By removing their preoccupation with the behaviour of the alcoholic they are able to focus on their own development and sense of identity.

Al-Anon meetings are held in 115 countries. There are over 24,000 Al-Anon groups worldwide.

Al-Anon: www.al-anon-ireland.org
Tel: Dublin (01) 8732699 and Cork (021) 4311899

laura

fair-weather husband

Laura* is a slim, attractive, friendly woman who has a practical attitude to life. She exudes confidence and competence. She grew up in a warm, loving family and has always had good, supportive friends. She doesn't think of herself as ambitious but she is hardworking and has been very successful in her career.

Laura did well in her exams at school but didn't go on to university after her Leaving Certificate because she was in a rush to grow up. She did a secretarial course and left Ireland to go and work in London. She came back from London after a few years and met an English man, Tony, while she was working in Dublin. He was working on contract, so when he went back home to Manchester Laura went with him. After a few years they got married and they enjoyed their early years together.

When they experienced problems conceiving a baby, Laura tried different fertility treatments without any success. Tony became uncommunicative and withdrew from Laura and their marriage eventually broke down.

I grew up in Dublin in the 1970s. I went to an all-girls Catholic school that was run by nuns. I enjoyed primary school; I was bright and I found it very easy. I have no horror stories about

* Names, occupations, locations and other identifying details have been altered to protect identities

unpleasant teachers, and I got good grades and reports. Secondary school was the same. It was just around the corner from the primary school and it was run by the same order of nuns. I had a nice group of friends in school and I'm still friends with people I knew when I was four.

I felt more grown up when I went to secondary school and did well academically. I always got good results. I was a great crammer and before my exams I'd cram all the information in, do the exam and then promptly forget it all.

My family is great; we all get on very well. I'm good friends with my siblings and the age differences matter less as we get older. My parents weren't too strict on us growing up. I was given a lot of freedom. They trusted me and I didn't let them down. It was a normal house. My dad worked full-time and my mum worked part-time. They both did shift work, so they were around the house at different times. They were good communicators and there was lots of open discussion about what was going on in our lives.

I had a few boyfriends in school but nothing serious or long-term. Some of the local guys in the area weren't nice so I stayed away from them. I did the Leaving Cert and it went well but I really wanted to get out in the world and work. I had no interest in going on to third level. My parents encouraged me to go to university and my siblings did go on to third level, but at the time it wasn't for me. After school I went to a secretarial college and did a course. I was impatient and I wanted my independence. Further study would have got in the way of that.

I liked doing the secretarial course because I was learning useful things. I knew when I finished I was going to have a tangible skill that would get me a job. After I completed the course I felt that I was very grown up and decided that I would go to London to work. I was just eighteen at the time.

My family had friends in London so they found me a house to stay in that was full of Irish people. The house was laid out in bedsits and had a shared kitchen. It was safe and secure and it was a better option for me than living alone. There were people around for a chat in the evenings and I got to know them and made friends.

I had a job organised before I went to London as a junior secretary in the head office of a big company. I thought it was brilliant. There were temps working there from all over the world and we had lots of fun. I met some nice guys and dated a bit.

I wanted to be busy at the weekends because I didn't know that many people, so I got a part-time job in a pub in Camden. I loved the pubs and the markets there. Maybe I'm looking back at that time through rose-tinted glasses but I think it was a great time in my life. I had lots of Irish friends dotted around London, sharing houses and staying in squats and we used to meet up and go to clubs and pubs. I'm sure there were lonely times but I genuinely don't remember them. After a while I decided that I didn't want to get stuck just hanging out with Irish people, so I made an effort to do different things and go to different places. I was very sociable and made friends easily through my two jobs in the office and the pub and I liked music, so I often went to the Camden Palace Club and to gigs and concerts.

I stayed in London for two years and then a few of my friends started going back home. I suddenly got a hankering for Ireland. It was the late 1980s and I was missing my family and my younger siblings, so I moved back home.

When I got home I'd changed a lot, so I found living with my parents was difficult; I liked my independence. After about nine months I moved into a flat on my own in Ranelagh. I had a good job that involved more administration than secretarial work, and things were going well. I was twenty-one and I was moving up the career ladder.

I walked in and out to work from Ranelagh to save on my bus fare and I lost a good bit of weight. I felt quite confident about how I looked in my twenties, but I didn't feel under any pressure to diet or anything like that. In those days there wasn't so much emphasis on how you looked. Everyone wore jeans and baggy jumpers at the weekend. It wasn't a big deal to be slim or to dress up and show off your cleavage. No one cared if you were a size ten, a twelve or a fourteen.

I have very good memories of Dublin during Italia '90. There were lots of parties at work and wild nights in pubs, where everyone was throwing pints in the air. It was the conception of the Celtic Tiger and there was a reckless, happy air in Dublin. I think Irish people were starting to become confident about themselves.

The changes in the economy affected my job and I was promoted and given more responsibility. I was in charge of setting up a new office and had a good salary. The next step was to a higher level and a company car. I didn't really see my job as a career because I hadn't had any expectations of a career. It was a job and it gave me enough money to support myself and go out and have a good time. I lived very much in the now. I was only interested in what was happening at the weekend. I did a few courses for work but I didn't think about further education. I wasn't interested in going to college as a mature student.

I was working in my new job for a year when Tony joined the company. He was brought over from the UK to work on a specific project. He was a skilled technician and was a few years older than me. We got on well and I thought he was lovely.

Tony had a girlfriend in England so at first we were just friends. He was funny and very fit and he had lovely long black hair. After he had been working in Ireland for two months, he came back from a trip to England and told me he'd broken up with his girlfriend. He asked me out and we started seeing each other regularly.

Tony was into sports in a big way. He played all kinds of sport but his favourite was rugby. I hadn't met any Irish guys who were rugby players or into team sports so it was interesting. He had a house he had bought in England and to me he seemed very together and grown up.

I went back and forth with him to his home in Manchester and met his family and friends. I stayed in his house and it was all very nice and easy. After his contract in Dublin was up he said he was going to move back to England and asked me if I wanted to come with him. I decided I would go. I didn't have a long-term plan – it was just the way I was living. It was spontaneous and it seemed like a good idea because we really enjoyed being together.

At first I didn't have a job when I moved over to Manchester so I was disorientated. Tony had to travel around Europe for work, so I was on my own for weeks at a time and that was hard at the start. His family was very friendly towards me and before long I got a temporary job and I settled down. I made a really good friend at my first job so I wasn't lonely for long.

Our relationship progressed and we worked on doing up Tony's house at the weekends. He was a very good builder and handyman and could turn his hand to anything. He'd bought the house as a wreck with the idea of fixing it up and selling it on. When it was done up, we decided we wanted a house that we both owned so he sold his house and we bought a nicer house together and renovated it and made it our own.

We got engaged and were married in 1994. I was twenty-six. We had a lovely Church of England wedding. I didn't mind that it wasn't Catholic. I don't have any great affinity with the Catholic Church and Tony was more religious than me. All my family and friends came over and everything went well. I suppose I was young getting married but I didn't feel that I was that young.

I felt secure with Tony and I thought we had a great future ahead of us. We had a blast on our honeymoon in Portugal. It was so much fun. We met another couple who were on honeymoon, too, and we all had a hoot.

When we came back from our honeymoon I applied for an administration job with a big British company. I got the job and it was a bit like getting into the civil service. It was a great company to work for; it had good pay and working conditions, and a pension plan.

I loved being married. I enjoyed being busy, organising our social lives and making our house a nice place to live. I felt secure in my job and I was learning how to drive. Tony was playing a lot of sport and we both had the time and the freedom to do the things we wanted to do.

When I was twenty-nine and Tony was thirty-two we started loosely talking about having kids. We didn't have a real plan to start immediately, but on my thirtieth birthday we said we would start trying.

I had always had an irregular cycle but I hadn't given it much thought. When we decided to start trying to have a baby I suddenly became very aware of our fertility and started to worry about my own. I thought I might have problems. I spoke to my doctor and she said to try for six months and see what happened. During that time my friend and my sister both got pregnant and I was very envious of them but I was only six months into trying so I wasn't massively worried.

After six months nothing was happening and things started to get more stressful. I felt that our love life was becoming mechanical for me, but Tony wasn't worried, so I don't think he knew how I was really feeling. I went back to the doctor and she recommended talking to someone in a fertility clinic. The great thing about fertility clinics in the UK is that the services are all free and easy to access. The doctors in the clinic were wonderful – they told me that I was OK and they couldn't find any real explanation for my infertility. They thought a hormone treatment would help to regulate things so they started me off on Clomid.

Clomid is used a lot to help regulate or induce ovulation. It's a pill that I had to take on certain days of my cycle. The clinic explained to me that they had to check if it was working by scanning me to see if I was ovulating, and if the drug wasn't working they would have to increase the dose. It helps a lot of people to get pregnant. They told me that 80 per cent of people who don't ovulate will ovulate with Clomid and that it was very effective.

I went through six cycles of Clomid over the next nine

months and still there was no baby. I was starting to get desperate. I discussed it with Tony and we went to the clinic together. They said we were both normal, everything was as it should be and that we should keep trying.

I really wanted a baby and not getting pregnant was making me want one even more. I am very family oriented and have always seen children as part of my life. I wanted to have my baby with Tony and he was well up for it too.

My career was progressing. I was being given more and more responsibility and my job involved making buying decisions and dealing with suppliers and marketing personnel. It was a surprise to me that I was getting a better salary and a company car was on the horizon because I didn't consider myself an ambitious person. I think I was 'accidentally ambitious'. I was beginning to think, 'Maybe I could have a successful career with this company.'

I could have pushed things in work to further my career but I didn't because I was very focused on having a baby. At one point I was going for scans every day at the clinic so the doctors could see if follicles were developing in my ovaries. It was very hard for them to figure out when I was ovulating so they were constantly monitoring me.

Tony wasn't keen on talking about the fertility treatments. He wasn't interested in discussing anything difficult. We hadn't had any bad times up until then so I didn't know how he was going to react. He liked the good things about our relationship – our social life, our house, having a good income together. When this challenge presented itself he clammed up and didn't think it was necessary to talk about it.

We were offered counselling as part of the fertility

treatment. It was free and compulsory for me. Tony never offered to go with me. I think he should have come but he told me that he couldn't talk to a stranger about it. He wasn't as open as me. I was getting more and more frustrated because some of our friends were getting pregnant and he was getting quieter and quieter about the situation. He was tuning out and concentrating on work and playing a lot of sport to relieve the stress.

The pressure of the fertility treatment was a new experience for me. I had no benchmark of how we were supposed to behave or react. I didn't know how much we should be talking about it. It is very grown-up stuff to deal with and we had to be very disciplined and organised about everything to do with our fertility and trying to get pregnant. Our lives became less spontaneous and more mechanical and objective.

In the end the fertility treatment took its toll on our relationship. I didn't realise how much or how seriously it was affecting us, because Tony didn't want to talk about it.

Tony had no fertility problems at all. In fact it was the opposite. Everything about him was perfect: motility, quality, everything. I was becoming increasingly aware that it was me that was causing the problem. I felt that it was my fault. Tony never said that to me. He never said the words: 'It's your problem' or 'It's your fault' but he was becoming detached. I felt that as we went on he was less interested and involved in the process. Things were tougher, and I didn't feel we were as close as we had been. It felt like we weren't in it together.

The clinic suggested we try intrauterine insemination (IUI) to help raise my chances of getting pregnant. It's used a lot when there appears to be no reason for infertility. I was given medication to help stimulate egg production and I was inseminated at the clinic when the time was right. While I was doing IUI I had to inject myself every day. It was very unpleasant. I was full of hormones and I wasn't myself. I felt like I had permanent PMT. I was sensitive, sore and my mood was low. It wasn't easy to carry on at home or at work as if everything was normal. I'd ring Tony each morning after I'd been to the hospital and tell him how things were going. He wouldn't really engage or seem very interested. He'd just say OK and that was it.

I think Tony just wanted to fix it. He was a practical person and he liked to fix things. He worked as a technician and if a machine had a problem he'd find out what it was and fix it. If there were things to renovate or do in the house, he could do them. The problem we had was that he was powerless. He couldn't do anything about my fertility and it was frustrating for him.

As time went on it seemed as if everyone in the world was getting pregnant incredibly easily. All they had to do was look at each other and they were pregnant. I had a heightened awareness of anything to do with babies. Every pram I saw on the street reminded me that I couldn't have a baby.

We did three courses of IUI, which took about a year in all. They didn't work. I was thirty-three and everything I'd tried had failed.

After the IUI failed, the next stage was to try in vitro fertilisation (IVF). This procedure is quite invasive as they remove your eggs and fertilise them in a test tube. I had to wait a few months to allow my system to settle down before we started it, and during that time things were getting much worse between Tony and me.

Tony had completely withdrawn from me and didn't want to discuss anything. There was a huge air of sadness in our house. I was very upset and I suppose I wasn't paying much attention to Tony. I had a great bunch of friends but I didn't like to bore them with my stories about the fertility treatments. I think my personality altered. I was so sad. I didn't realise how much I'd changed until afterwards, when it was all over.

I was upset all the time and every month, when I realised that I wasn't pregnant, it was hell. I felt as if I was drowning in a never-ending cycle of trying to get pregnant and then being disappointed. I couldn't get out of it physically or emotionally and all I was looking forward to was more of the same. It was overwhelming, but I deeply wanted to keep charging ahead with it. I felt that the problem was my fault and if only I was 'normal' everything would be OK.

I wasn't expressing my sadness by crying all the time, but I was low. It was affecting our social life and I remember missing certain events around that time which wasn't like me. I didn't go to a wedding or a hen weekend because I didn't want to drink and I was in bad form. The struggle to get pregnant was affecting everything.

I didn't like being where I was emotionally and physically but it was where I had to be. When you speak to other people who are going through the same thing they understand. People who aren't going through it think you're crazy. They can't relate or empathise. I think you can say that about a lot of tough experiences that people go through. You have to do it before you can really understand it.

Tony was coming home from work later and later. He was normally home at six but it became eight or nine o'clock and then even later. I don't think he wanted to come home at all. I was getting worried. I had a feeling he was avoiding talking to me by staying out late and spending as little time as possible with me. He was throwing himself into sports and he was training one rugby team and playing for another, so he had two sets of matches and training sessions every week. He wasn't drinking or anything like that; he was just playing a huge amount of sport.

Tony came home late one Friday evening. I'd been calling him on his mobile because I was expecting him earlier and he didn't answer. He came in when it was too late for dinner. We were hardly talking, but then he said, 'It's not working, so I'm going.' He went into our room and packed his bags. I tried to talk to him but he left.

I think he had been working up to it for a while but had chickened out of telling me he wanted to leave. I was very upset so I called a friend and she came over and stayed the night with me. I didn't think Tony had gone for good. I thought he was having a crisis and we could get over it if we talked about it. I knew it was going to be difficult because he wasn't a talker.

Tony didn't come from a family that was open or that talked about their feelings or what was happening in their lives. They were very superficial and their conversations were banal. They'd prefer to talk about the weather than a problem they were having. His parents and siblings weren't communicative on the level that I was used to. I'm not making excuses for him but he had no role model from his parents about how to communicate in a relationship.

I tried to call Tony the next day but he didn't respond. I took some time off work and booked a flight back to Ireland on my seventh wedding anniversary. I rang my mother and my sister and they said that it would be fine. They thought it was a tiff and we'd get over it. They knew we'd both been unhappy about the fertility treatments and that we were disappointed that we couldn't have a baby.

I didn't know what was happening. I didn't know if he'd really left. Was it real or not? It's like when someone dies and you can't accept it. I stayed with my parents for a week and we analysed it, overanalysed it and analysed it again. The general consensus from everyone was that it was a glitch and we'd get over it and it wouldn't end our marriage.

Looking back on it now I think that Tony had been seeing someone else for a long time. He had to have had a girlfriend because I think he was too weak to leave me without having someone to go to. He wouldn't tell me where he was living or who he was living with.

I talked to Tony briefly on the phone from Ireland and he asked me when I was coming back. He said he would pick me up from the airport when I came back after the week at home. That gave me some hope and I thought we'd have an opportunity to talk things through. But when I got to arrivals he wasn't there. A friend of mine was there to meet me. Tony had called her and asked her to meet me instead. When I got back to the house, all his stuff was gone. That was an awful shock. I still didn't think that it was over and I thought we were going to talk. I didn't know what to do next.

I didn't want to stay in the house on my own so I went to stay with a friend. It was September 11, 2001, and I remember looking at the events in New York on television and feeling numb. It felt surreal because I couldn't respond normally. I think I had overdosed on pain and I had no capacity for any more. I knew that it was upsetting for people all over the world but I was crying for myself and not for them.

I had to gather my strength and move back into our house after a few days. I didn't like being on my own in the beginning but after a few nights I was OK. My boss in work was fantastic. She knew that I'd been doing the fertility treatment and I'd told her that it hadn't worked and things were very sad at home. I hadn't let it get in the way of my work, but she understood I was going through a hard time. When Tony left, she told me I could take some time off. I think she considered it compassionate leave. I was off work for three weeks and it wasn't discussed when I went back. I was paid and it wasn't taken out of my holidays. I'm sure my doctor would have signed a note if I'd asked her to. I wasn't suffering from depression – it was very intense grief. It was like Tony had died but it was worse because he was still alive. This person who had been such an intrinsic part of my life was gone. I didn't know where he was or what he was doing.

I had to pick myself up and get on with my work. I was still depositing my cheques into our joint account and so was Tony. There was no issue about money. I made a list of our outgoings and I divided everything up. I organised things so that he contributed towards the mortgage and insurance and I paid some of the other bills. I wanted to be independent so I said to him, 'This is my house for now; you're not to come here.'

I went through the gamut of emotions during this time. I was full of anger in the beginning and then disbelief, pain and loss. The only good thing about him leaving was that I didn't have to go through any more fertility treatments. I also had a lot of free time. I wasn't cooking or coming home early any more. I joined a gym and got fit and after six weeks I started to feel OK. I think that because we didn't have any children I slipped into my new single life very easily.

After five or six months I was feeling a lot stronger. My job was going well, I didn't have any financial concerns because we were splitting the mortgage and mentally I was getting stronger. My friends were good to me. I travelled to Thailand, I went to language classes and dated a bit. It was scary dating new guys because I'd been with the same person for ten years.

After I came back from Thailand Tony got in touch. He came around to the house and said to me, 'I love you. I want you. What can I do to get back with you?' I suspected that his relationship was in trouble. He seemed desperate – maybe the grass wasn't as green on the other side as he thought it would be. He wanted us to get back together and not discuss anything that had happened since we broke up.

I wasn't tempted to get back with him in the slightest. I didn't think he meant it. I didn't think he was 100 per cent sincere. I thought he wanted his old life and home back. It wasn't that he wanted me.

I was still seeing the counsellor that I'd started seeing for the fertility treatment even though we weren't talking about fertility any more. It really helped me to have an impartial person to speak to at that time. She was also trained as a marriage counsellor and she told me that it was very common for marriages to fall apart because of infertility.

Tony asked if he could come along to see the counsellor with me. It was awful. He was really angry and I was very strong. I said that I didn't think we would get back together again. I saw that under the anger he was falling apart but he couldn't say anything. He didn't give the counselling a chance. He sat there with his arms folded. I think I went to the counselling with him because I felt sorry for him, not because I thought it would help us get back together again.

After that I felt I had more control of my identity and my life. I'd changed my surname to Tony's name after we got married because it had been important to him, so I changed back to my maiden name by deed poll. I negotiated our separation and we lived apart without any disagreements. I wasn't trying to have a baby any more, so I wasn't being controlled by my body and my lack of fertility. I was back to the person I used to be and it felt good.

I saw Tony on and off. He was calling me and trying to get in touch. A few months after the counselling disaster he asked me to go out on a date with him. He said, 'Let's try it once and see how it goes.' I don't know why I went, maybe part of me wanted to try so I went out with him for the day. It felt like we were two friends who had nothing to say to each other. At one point he tried to hold my hand and it felt awful. I pulled away from him. When he dropped me home that evening I told him it was definitely over.

Occasionally I was getting phone calls at night and the person who was calling would hang up. One day Tony called over to see me and while he was there in the house with me the phone rang and a woman on the end of the phone said to me, 'I know he's been calling around to see you, but

I'm with him now. I can give him what you can't.' She then told me that she was living with Tony and he had got her pregnant and made her have an abortion. She sounded mad and I knew that couldn't be true as Tony wasn't like that. I said to her, 'Leave me alone. Tony's gone from my life; he doesn't live here any more, and this is my home. So stop ringing me.' Tony heard the conversation because I'd put it on speaker and he said to me: 'That's why I'm leaving her. She's an absolute nutter.'

I was furious with him. He was actually looking to me for sympathy because his affair hadn't worked out. I had the phone in my hand and I was so annoyed I threw it at his head. It hit him quite hard and he was shocked. I said, 'Get out now. I don't want you calling in here any more. This is absolutely my place.' Then he said, 'Can I come and cut the grass sometimes?' He was still looking for a reason, any reason, to keep seeing me. I still loved an element of him but at that moment I thought he was pathetic and I couldn't understand why I'd ever gone out with him or married him.

After two years we got divorced and Tony bought me out of the house. I got three valuations and we took an average of them and we split the value between us. I bought a wreck of a house with the settlement and did it up. Tony came over with his friends and renovated the bathroom and installed central heating. I was very specific about what I wanted and he had to do it at the weekends or when I wasn't there. He did it out of guilt and I knew that, and it felt right. I spent the year making the house nice and planting a garden. It was a great project for me; it was healing.

Tony made the application to divorce me and I was happy to agree with everything he proposed. We had divided up our possessions by going around the house together and deciding ourselves what we wanted. I think it was a very even split. I didn't bother getting a lawyer because I was happy that it was fair. The judge asked to speak to me in her chambers because she was concerned that I hadn't got any legal advice. Once she knew that I was comfortable with the agreement and hadn't been put under any pressure, she made an absolute decree for our divorce. We decided that we weren't going to affect each other's pensions. I was happy with that because I didn't want anything that would tie us together in the future.

I started saving and booked time off work to go on a big trip to Australia. I had always wanted to go but Tony had never been interested. I planned to take three months off and travel around Australia and New Zealand.

That year I was in Ireland for my Christmas holidays and had booked my flights to Australia for February. A gang of friends from Dublin had rented a house in Kerry for New Year's Eve and I was joining them. My friends told me that a guy called Jamie was coming along and that he was really nice. They said that they thought I'd get on well with him, that he was quiet but he had a really good, sarky sense of humour.

Jamie and I did get on well. He was funny and had great one-liners. I really liked him. We went for a walk on the beach and talked a bit and he held my hand for a second but nothing happened. He drove me home from Kerry with another friend but he had to drop me off first and I was disappointed because I really liked him and wanted to spend more time with him.

I went back to Dublin for a weekend at the end of January

and went out with the same group of friends to a restaurant in town. Jamie came along. He didn't know I was going to be there and I didn't know he was going to be there – it was a total set-up! We got on brilliantly and we stayed out late and chatted for ages. We found out about each other's pasts. I had recently got divorced and he had just come out of a very long relationship six months before. I was going away two weeks later so we said we'd keep in touch and see how it went. I didn't want to be his rebound relationship.

We spoke every day while I was travelling and when I came home in May I decided that I wanted to come home to live in Ireland. Ten months after we met I sold my house in Manchester. Jamie helped me move all my stuff and we started living together as soon as I got back. It all happened quite fast but it felt right.

We got married two years after we met. I was thirty-eight and he was forty-two. I'd told Jamie that I had fertility problems and he said that it didn't matter if we never had children, that he would be happy with me. He knew I didn't want to go through all that again. I thought the process was very destructive and I was adamant that I was through with it. After we were married for a few months Jamie said to me, 'I really think you should give it one more try if you want to be a mother. It would be a shame if you didn't.'

I was very nervous about the idea. It took me a year before I made an appointment with a clinic in Dublin. We went along to meet the doctor in September and he said that he would start a course of treatment for IVF in January. We both decided to relax before we started and enjoy our few months of freedom. We'd booked our summer holidays late and went to France in September. We had a great time.

We drank lots of red wine and ate lovely food. I completely chilled out.

When we got back I was feeling very sore and out of sorts. For some reason I decided I'd do a pregnancy test and for the first time ever it was positive. I burst into tears and told Jamie and he couldn't believe it. We were both in a state of total disbelief. We weren't jumping around or celebrating – we were too shocked. It was only after we had our twelve-week scan that I actually accepted that I was pregnant. It was real and it was wonderful. I'm so happy now that we didn't miss out on it. It's lovely to have a child.

Tony is with someone else now and he has two daughters. He's still friends with some of my friends but I don't ask them about him. I'm not curious and I don't want to know about him.

It's difficult to compare relationships. I'm a different person now from the person I was when I was twenty-one. I was young and I was having fun. My relationship with Jamie is much more grown up. It's nice and it's comfortable. Both our families are the same – they're open and communicative. They talk about what's going on in their lives and we're happy to be living in Ireland and both lucky enough to have jobs.

Jamie and I both had relationships that didn't work out and that went on too long. When I look back I don't think of Tony as a grown-up person. He was a fair-weather husband – there for the good times but not able to cope when I needed him to support me emotionally. I think that if we'd encountered any other difficulties it would have been the same. If I'd been ill or needed to talk about difficult stuff he wouldn't have been there for me. With Jamie I feel secure, I know we are there for each other 100 per cent through the good times and the bad, and right now, with our child, it's good times.

❋ ❋ ❋

Fertility Treatment

Infertility is defined as the inability to conceive after trying for one year. It's estimated that one in six couples in Ireland have difficulty conceiving.

There are a number of private clinics in Ireland that can help. Human Assisted Reproduction Ireland (HARI), based at the Rotunda Hospital in Dublin, is the largest centre in Ireland. It opened in 1989 and is self-funding and non-profit-making. It sees about 1,500 people a year. HARI offers many different types of treatments for patients, including Follicle Tracking, Intrauterine Insemination, In Vitro Fertilisation and Gamete Cryopreservation.

American fertility experts have studied the effects of stress on reproduction. There is no clear link between stress and fertility but they have found that pregnancy is more likely to occur during months when couples are feeling happy and relaxed and less likely to occur when they are tense and anxious. Many doctors recommend that women use alternative therapies such as acupuncture and massage while they are trying fertility treatments.

Counsellors are available to meet fertility treatment patients in the Rotunda every day, free of charge.

HARI: www.hari.ie
Tel: (01) 8072732

❋ ❋ ❋

david

your father for ever

David* is an incredibly open, intelligent man who speaks eloquently and philosophically about the awful aftermath of his relationship breakdown.

He met his Russian wife, Veronika, on the internet, and after a whirlwind romance she moved to Ireland. He became a stepfather to her daughter, Alena, but never adopted her.

Veronika had an affair and then decided she wanted to go back to Russia, and it took David two years to sort out their separation. Sadly, he had to say goodbye to his daughter, Alena, because he had no parental rights when their relationship ended.

My name is David. I grew up in Dublin in a big family. I had four sisters and I was the only boy. My mother and father were both architects. I was a very small kid and was really shy. I grew up in a house full of women, so I didn't get the whole 'male' thing. My dad was artistic and he wasn't a classic alpha-male role model.

I don't remember very well but I think I was bullied a bit in my first junior school. I liked my second junior school because it was co-ed and the gender mix seemed more normal to me. There was this weird world of male/male

---

*Names, occupations, locations and other identifying details have been altered to protect identities.

relationships going on in all-boys schools. The way boys hung out together and talked together fascinated me but I felt like I wasn't getting it. I was taken out of one of my schools because I lacked confidence as a child. My confidence got a bit shot by people around me who were way more confident than me.

There were a couple of incidents when I was a kid where I caused my parents no end of panic. I remember going to friends' houses and telling their parents that I was allowed to stay the night when I wasn't. I think I did that because I enjoyed getting attention and space in other people's homes. In my house there were always women talking together and I was shy about myself, so their problems seemed to take precedence over mine.

I think that like a lot of families of that time we weren't great at communicating with each other on an emotional level. It was considered a bit odd if you were trying to do that, and the ones in my family who did were considered to be the overemotional, weepy ones.

I never took to the all-male environment – I wasn't at home in the culture that existed at my senior school, which was a conservative, Catholic, all-boys school. There were lots of boys there who were children of my parents' friends. They were model students and model sportsmen. They were held up to me as examples and I think that pushed me permanently to the periphery. They were everything I was never going to be. I didn't like rugby and I wasn't performing academically in what was a very competitive environment.

I loved art but it wasn't encouraged in my school. I was used to my co-ed non-denominational junior school with a mixed bag of people and I couldn't put myself into the context of a conservative Catholic environment. I fizzled out and ended up with a poor Leaving Cert.

After that I worked for seven years in a bar. Eventually I was made the manager, but I was smart enough to realise that if I didn't do something about it this was as far as I was going to go.

Fortunately for me my dad spotted that I was in trouble and he suggested I do a course for architectural technicians. This was exactly the right thing for me at the time. I loved it and after a while I decided I wanted to do architecture.

It became obvious to me that I needed re-sit my Leaving Cert to get into architecture in UCD. So I sat physics, maths, English and art, and when I was twenty-six I went to UCD as a mature student to study architecture.

That was the most incredible experience of my life. Before I went to college I thought that I had got to a point in my life where 'this was it', but suddenly I felt I was beginning to achieve something. Suddenly there were ten roads in front of me instead of just one.

College was incredibly easy in one way and incredibly difficult in another. I found it easy to achieve a balance and to get good results. Being in the working world had given me the ability to set myself targets and achieve them. But emotionally I found college difficult. I had lots of friends but I was a bit uneasy and felt uncomfortable. I probably appeared more confident than I was. I socialised a lot but felt shy and had to push myself.

I was meeting and dating lots of girls. They liked that I was older and quite sophisticated compared with the younger students. I found it easier to get on with women because I was more comfortable and relaxed with them.

They were much easier to understand than men for me, which I suppose is understandable when you have four sisters. I was clean, sober and interested in talking. And because I didn't exhibit the usual alpha-male behaviours, girls weren't threatened by me.

I didn't fall in love at that time because I was like a kid in a sweet shop. There was so much choice. That was great but I was stressed out at the same time. It was as if I was going through a late adolescence. I think I had closed in on myself and shut down a bit while I was in school, and now that I was in college I started to allow myself to feel and express myself, and that process was painful.

I got involved in my first serious relationship when I finished college. She was an architect as well and we ended up working and living together. I started off in the relationship by being very attentive but after a while I withdrew and became quite passive aggressive. I think if I become unsure in a relationship I pull down the shutters and stop communicating. I would still be around my girlfriend but I wouldn't talk and I think that silence can be quite intimidating.

I only realise I did this by looking back at the situation from my present perspective. At the time I had no idea I was doing it. My girlfriend wasn't great at expressing herself either. She never told me I was behaving badly or discussed what we should do. I think she just tolerated what was going on and didn't react. Eventually she withdrew as well and the relationship petered out.

After that I became involved in a lot of difficult, short-term relationships. I was feeling awkward about women and commitment. I was single and tired of meeting up with people at parties, bars and clubs. But I wasn't over my ex and I felt that I didn't have anything to give anyone and I didn't want to get into anything serious. It all seemed so complicated.

I'd heard a lot of friends in work talking about internet dating and cybersex. I thought it would be a great way to meet someone. I loved the idea of specifically engineering a situation where I'd be able to talk to someone without ever meeting them. I was looking for a virtual one-night stand where I could find some kind of connection, while at the same time knowing that, as a relationship, it was going nowhere.

I think that's the huge draw and the huge problem with internet dating. It's so easy to set yourself up on the net and meet people and then you can morally wash your hands because you haven't actually done anything. You're able to connect with someone emotionally without having to take them out or make a physical connection. It's a way of getting support from someone or getting involved in each other's lives with very little effort and no commitment. You don't have to leave your house – you can be involved and completely detached at the same time.

Veronika was Russian and lived in Saint Petersburg. We first contacted each other through a singles' dating website. I saw her photo on her profile and I thought she was gorgeous, very dramatic looking. We immediately connected with each other in a chat room and started sending each other emails. We talked about all the kinds of things you would talk to a girl about in a bar or at a party if you were sober. She had a really dark sense of humour and I can be a bit of a bitch as well, so I felt like I'd met someone whose humour matched mine.

We started phoning each other after about ten days of emailing. We were having a conversation one night on the phone when she asked me what I was doing for the weekend and I told her that I had nothing planned. I asked her what she was going to do and she said she was going to this amazing ballet. I started to wonder what the fuck I was doing in Ireland without her. I said that to her and she said, 'Why don't you come over?'

I booked a flight to Saint Petersburg the next day. When we met in the airport we were both so excited. We were all over each other in the taxi. It all seemed so strange and unreal. On the phone we had been getting quite explicit with each other and you're not sure if there's going to be any chemistry when you actually meet, but it was there in spades.

We had two amazing weeks together in Saint Petersburg. We went to all the galleries, saw all the sights and spent lots of time with her daughter, Alena. She was only six months old and her father was some idiot alcoholic who had disappeared from her life.

I didn't know much about Veronika's background. She was quite secretive about it. She was living on her own in an apartment with her daughter, and her family was supporting her. Her lifestyle seemed OK. She had trained as a ballerina when she was young and she looked after herself and cared about her appearance. She wasn't well educated in that she hadn't gone to college and didn't have a degree, but she had lots of books and art in her apartment and was very well read, so I felt we were on the same level intellectually.

After our romantic two weeks together I came back to

Ireland and Veronika was planning to come over to visit me in the summer for two weeks. Neither of us could wait that long, so she came over after two months. We decided while she was over that she would move here permanently with Alena.

People thought I was nuts but I really didn't care. I'd spent so much of my life not committing to anyone and being afraid of any kind of commitment or decision-making that I just thought 'fuck it', and I went for it.

I had really strong feelings for Veronika and we got on so well that I knew it was the right thing to do. We had this incredible connection. We shared the same sense of humour, we had the same eclectic taste in architecture, music and film, we both shared a weird mix of urban and rural passions – we just got on really well together.

Veronika went back to Russia and sorted things out and then she moved over to Ireland for good. She didn't need a visa to move here. She had a holiday visa and we discovered that once you tell the Department of Foreign Affairs that you're planning to get married they will extend your visa.

We decided to get married that Christmas. People were surprised but they knew I was impulsive and romantic so they were happy for me. I had no doubts and was completely swept away by her and thought our relationship was fantastic. I was sure that we were doing the right thing.

I was working for myself at the time and I was pretty busy. One year into our marriage we moved to Waterford because I was working on a big housing project. Around the time we made the move we discovered that Alena was deaf. My mother had suspected there was a problem when she was about a year old. She was honest with me and suggested that I have her tested.

We brought Alena to see two public health nurses, both of whom said that she was fine. We knew she wasn't fine so the third time we had her screened privately. There was an American doctor who held a clinic in Ireland once a month and we brought Alena to see him. He immediately diagnosed her as being severely deaf.

The first thing you think of when your daughter is diagnosed with a disability is, 'What will happen to her when I'm gone? Will she be able to get a job? Who will look after her?'

There was never a disconnect between Alena and me apart from her hearing problems. I was always good with kids and when I fell in love with Veronika, Alena was part of the deal. It was easy to be a family because Alena's father had abdicated his responsibilities, so there was a space for me to fill.

After her diagnosis Alena became the main focus of our relationship. We were very upset in the beginning and then we got really organised about it and found out the best way that she could be treated. We discovered that she could have an operation to get a cochlear implant, in Beaumont Hospital, and that she would need speech therapy to help her catch up.

I don't think Alena's problems affected our social life initially but they didn't do our relationship any good, and I think they masked the stress in our relationship because she became the focal point.

My career was going fine at that point. I had a good income but I was working incredibly long hours. Veronika had talked me into the idea of buying a very big house, which we were going to renovate and sell. While we were living there she didn't have a job apart from taking care of Alena. She was supposed to be helping me do up the house and supervise the building work but that didn't happen. She didn't do a huge amount of housework either. She would tidy up a bit, but I did all the cooking, shopping and a lot of the cleaning.

Veronika was really into horses and she wanted to teach riding and do dressage. Eventually I gave in and bought her a horse. She entered lots of shows but she didn't teach anyone to ride and her hobby didn't generate any income.

I didn't really care whether she worked or not from an income point of view, but it frustrated me that she didn't have the drive to do something with her life. My mother had always worked with my father in his practice and I saw that it made a huge difference to her to have a purpose and a passion outside of the family. I thought that Veronika needed something apart from Alena and me to be passionate about.

Life took its toll on us and we spent less and less time together. Instead of talking through our problems we lost our way. Veronika seemed depressed and had no motivation. I tried hard to stimulate her and I packed her off to horse shows every week hoping that she would be energised by something new. It was while she was at one of those horse shows that she met Michael and started an affair with him.

I knew immediately that Veronika was having an affair – it was very obvious. She became much quieter, uncommunicative and very detached. She also started getting text messages all the time. Previously she had been really bad about keeping her phone with her. I would always be at her to remember to take it with her, and suddenly she wouldn't let it out of her sight. I drove myself nuts for about a month, thinking about what was happening. She kept saying the calls were all about the horse shows or the horses but I knew she was lying.

Veronika went to Saint Petersburg with Alena for two weeks' holiday with her parents while all this was going on. During that time I went to a therapist for some help. I couldn't handle knowing about this affair and having her calmly deny it and tell me I was nuts.

Veronika and I sat down when they came back and I went through everything that was going on with her. She got very upset and didn't want to talk about us anymore, full stop, end of story. My therapist had told me to be patient and gave me techniques to deal with the situation. Veronika became really evasive for the next few months – there were all kinds of contradictions in her behaviour.

My therapist said to me that I had to keep asking the questions and that when the actions matched the words I would be getting somewhere. Her behaviour was not matching her words so I didn't believe anything she said. He also said that you should never believe something that your partner says when there is emotion in their voice. When they sit down with you and tell you in a calm manner that the relationship is over, then they are telling you the truth.

On my birthday I realised that it was over. Veronika tried to get me to take the day off work to look after Alena so that she could spend time with Michael. She had completely forgotten about my birthday. I asked her calmly what was going on and she told me calmly that it was over.

I spent the next four to five months in a kind of limbo.

I wasn't depressed; I was in turmoil. I'd never experienced so much shock, confusion and loss and I was very close to falling apart. My family had never seen me so traumatised and they were very worried about me.

I sat Veronika down every few nights and asked her the same questions: 'Do you love me? Do you want this marriage to work? Are you prepared to work on our problems?' Eventually she said: 'No, I don't want this marriage to work any more.' I'd been so terrified for such a long time of finding out the truth that it was a huge relief just to have it out there.

At this stage Veronika still hadn't admitted to the affair. I went into her mobile phone account and looked at her bills one evening. I knew exactly who he was and what was going on but she continued to pretend that Michael was just a friend. I still wanted to fix things but she wanted out. Every time she was a little honest with me, she would follow it by lying again and I couldn't trust her.

Trust is like a glass vessel. If it breaks once and the pieces are big enough you can put it back together. But if you take those bits and break them again, then eventually they will get so small that you will be left with lots of tiny shards. You won't know where or how to start putting them back together again. If she hadn't broken all the pieces so badly I think we would still be together.

In one email to her friend in Russia, Veronika said that I was kind and generous, and she was lucky to have me but that I could be very quiet sometimes. A month later she sent another email to him, saying that I was cold and manipulative and she thought I had never loved her.

She was very manipulative when I pushed her to make a decision about staying in the marriage. She told me that she couldn't make the decision because she was vulnerable, living in another country and she had to sort out all the problems that we had with Alena's hearing. My counsellor said that was rubbish.

Veronika never admitted to the affair so our relationship became impossible. I had completely lost trust in her at that stage and we talked about separating. I think she was afraid to actually say she had had an affair because she thought it might affect her settlement if we divorced, but she knew that I knew. In the end I was the one who actually pushed for the separation. She suggested we try to reconcile but I don't believe she really wanted to.

Once the proceedings started I felt she was being greedy about what she wanted. She said that she'd heard on radio programmes that as my wife she was entitled to half of everything I had. She started to get very demanding about property. We had an apartment in Spain that was rented out and she said that I had to put it in her name.

I asked several people for advice and I decided to call three solicitors that friends had recommended. I spoke to all of them and picked one woman who I liked. I chose her because she was very focused and pragmatic and seemed to understand what I wanted to do and how I wanted to do it. I wanted to settle things but I wasn't going to roll over. It took a year of negotiating before we reached a settlement. There were lots of letters going back and forth and I talked to Veronika from time to time about how things were going.

While the lawyers were sending letters, a friend of mine said: 'You ought to decide between the two of you what you want and tell the lawyers what you have agreed, otherwise you will be using your lawyers as weapons rather than interpreters.' I thought that was good advice.

While we were negotiating the separation, the property market was going downhill fast and I don't think Veronika realised what was happening. She was convinced that I had a stash of money hidden away somewhere and that I was going to hand over half a million to her to settle. I gave her an affidavit of means, which listed all my assets and expenses. She didn't believe the affidavit and I felt hers was wrong too.

From the questions she was asking my lawyer and me I sensed that she wanted to go home to Russia. She realised that without me paying all the bills and supporting her that things weren't going to be easy. I had very mixed emotions about this. In some ways I thought it might be good for Alena to get to know all her relations in Russia. She didn't mix with mine much because she spoke Russian better than English and Veronika didn't get on with my family and didn't allow Alena to see my sisters or my parents. And part of me wanted Veronika gone because she had become so mercenary.

The problem was that I was devastated about Alena. I had gone for counselling and discussed the fact that I felt Veronika was using her as a pawn. She tried to say to me that if I didn't give her enough money that she'd have to go back to Russia and I'd never see Alena again. One night she said to Alena: 'It will be sad when we go back home to Russia because Daddy won't be able to visit us very often.' I pulled her up on it and she said that it was better for her to get used to the idea that I wouldn't be around all the time. I decided then that I could never trust her again because she was using our child as a weapon to force me to give her as much money as possible. There was no point in fighting with her, because she wanted to go back to Russia and I had absolutely no rights as I hadn't adopted Alena.

I thought it was a cruel irony that after seven years of living together, and continuing to be in her life while the separation was being dealt with, that she had a right to a share of my property but I wasn't entitled to any recognition as a parent at all. My lawyer confirmed that that was exactly the case. It was open and shut. I had absolutely no right to have any role in Alena's life. I had fully intended to adopt her but it was one of those things that we never got around to. It was and is a source of great regret to me.

It took two years to sort things out and during that time I saw Alena as much as I could. I was living in a friend's house some of the time so I could get some space. In the end I gave Veronika a lump sum and she went back to Russia. I think she must have had some money squirreled away because she bought a place when she got back there.

The most upsetting thing I ever had to do in my life was to say goodbye to Alena. When I was walking through the airport with her I could feel her hand tightening on mine, and her whole body was tense because she knew what was happening and where she was going. We stopped and we both started crying and hugging each other. It was heartbreaking and one of the few times that I ever saw her cry.

I've spoken to Alena on the phone a few times since they left. It's difficult. I think it's the mix of her hearing problem and the fact that she's growing up. I'm sure her mother isn't painting me as a saint either. I don't know if she's saying bad things about me, but she must be pissed off with me. Alena probably thinks that I left her.

When I look back I think that Alena benefited hugely from being in Ireland. She got the best treatment for her hearing problem and I loved being a parent to her. She's now doing really well and is in mainstream education.

My father said to me that there are people who spend their entire lives trying to make a meaningful difference in someone's life and they never manage to do it. I like to think that over the years I spent with Alena I transformed her life. So how can you regret anything about that? No matter how negative the feelings are I am able to see that as a positive outcome from everything that happened.

I hope I'll see Alena again. Friends have advised me to write off the relationship and let it pass, stop chasing it and let it go. People say to me that she's not my daughter and I should forget it. But I still send her the latest girly toys and clothes and I'm her friend on Facebook. I've provided for her in my will and set up a fund for her education. I hope that at some stage, when she's older, that she'll realise that I want to keep the lines of communication open.

I wrote a letter to Alena as part of my counselling. I can't read it without getting upset. That moment of letting someone go is so powerful and I had to acknowledge that I could do nothing about her going. Life does some weird shit to you and you can't struggle against it. I've stopped being angry with Veronika and the letter I wrote to Alena is about me and her, not about me and her mother.

> Dear Alena,
>
> I'm writing you this letter not knowing whether you will ever receive it or not. Right now your mother and I are starting the process of separating, and since I'm not sure how things will go, I decided to sit down and write

you a letter to explain how I feel and what's happening right now. If you do get this letter in the future, please know that I love you. I tried hard to be there for you but it might turn out that I couldn't. Just remember that I didn't have the choice about what is happening now. It's not what I want to happen and I'm really sad about that. But remember most of all that of all of the things that have happened to me in my life, you're the one thing that I look back on with huge pride, great love and a lot of happiness.

When I first met you, your mother and I were in love. I had decided that I would never have children of my own. I always liked kids but thought that I'd never have the patience or commitment to be a good parent. You came as part of the deal with your mother. I didn't regret it – you were such a happy baby that I couldn't but love you. I remember when you were so small that I used to worry about you not being able to handle the cold when we went back to Russia. I remember you starting to walk and I remember you playing the piano in my parents' house.

When you came to Ireland, my thoughts changed to thinking about your future. Once your mother and I got married, my whole being was focused on our future as a family. All I thought about was building a home and financial stability that would look after us until we would grow old and die. Looking back on things, maybe I spent too much time doing that and not enough trying to build the marriage with your mother.

When you were about two, you were diagnosed with hearing problems. My mother was instrumental in having the diagnosis done, and she really cared about you and wanted to make sure that you got whatever intervention was available. For your mother it was hard, as the diagnosis was something that would inevitably confirm that something wasn't right.

Myself and your mother were confused, scared and worried for us all. We didn't know what that meant for you or for us but at that stage you found it difficult to communicate with us. It was very hard for us and I'm sure that it was just as hard for you then and since. I remember coming home from a few days away one day and as I came into the room, you ignored me, oblivious to my return. I was sad about this because I was worried about how your hearing difficulties were affecting you.

Once the diagnosis happened, we worked very hard to try and understand what it meant and what could be done to help you. Over the next year or two, a miracle happened and you had a great operation, which gave you a cochlear implant. You started to interact more and more, and then one day you began to exchange words with us and that was the start of what I can only describe as a transformation.

Since then, you have developed to the stage that now you are becoming indistinguishable from any other child your age. The only difference is that you are brighter, smarter and better in lots of ways than them. I am so proud to have been with you on this journey, and I know that maybe as that journey ends for me, it is certainly only beginning for you.

You now have the whole world ahead of you. The worry I once had for you is now replaced by my hopes and dreams that you will fulfil your own dreams and that makes me so happy. I may never know what you turn out to become, but I know that you will now have the chance to achieve what I once thought of as impossible for you, and for that alone I feel that my life has not been wasted.

You mother has decided to end this marriage. I tried to save it but for reasons you and I may never fully understand, she decided to leave. I am really sad about this because it is a double blow for me to lose you both. I treasure every moment with the two of you right now, knowing that I don't have many of them left. I thought that when this moment came it would be because I was dying, I never thought it would happen so soon.

Not being your birth father, I have no rights of access to you under Irish law. This means that despite my love for you and the strong bond that exists between us, I have no right to demand that it continues. This hurts incredibly. My heart is torn apart by the fear of losing you. I feel like a man condemned to death, knowing that I may only have a small amount of time left with you. I sat on your bed this morning watching you sleep. I cried for a while, feeling on one hand very sad and on the other realising that the feeling was because I was alive and because I did love you. You will never know how hard it was not to just take you in my arms and carry you away with me somewhere where I can be with you and not be separated.

Tonight you asked me what makes people cry, I told you it was because they are sad or hurt. You then asked me what makes you happy, and when I told you, you asked me what makes me happy. I told you that you did. Then you asked me what makes me the happiest and I told you that you did. You turned to me and said 'Thank you, Dad.' With those three words I was the happiest and luckiest person to ever have lived.

Alena, you mean the world to me. I now realise that you are for me the reason I was put on this world. As sad as I am that we may part and not see each other again, I hope that at some stage you will want to try and find me. If you choose to do this, you should know that you will find an open door and open arms awaiting you.

Your loving father,
David

⁂

The Adoption Authority of Ireland

The Adoption Authority of Ireland was established in 2010. It works to improve the standards of domestic and inter-country adoption. The regulatory framework around adoption has been strengthened to try to ensure that the best interests of the child are protected throughout the adoption process. Inter-country adoptions are accepted in Ireland with countries that have ratified the Hague Convention or with countries where Ireland has a bilateral agreement.

Step-parent Adoption: A step-parent adoption is where a child is adopted by one of its natural parents and the spouse of that parent who is not the natural parent. Usually it's the natural mother and her husband. A step-parent adoption gives the spouse of the natural parent legal rights within the family and protects the child's inheritance rights.

When the application for adoption is made by the natural parent and his or her spouse, they make the application to adopt together. This is because the natural parent gives up his or her sole rights and shares them with his or her spouse.

Children that are born within a previous marriage aren't eligible for adoption. It's usually an application that's made where the child is not in contact with his or her other natural parent. If the birth father is a legally appointed guardian of the child his consent must be obtained. If he isn't a guardian then he must be notified and consulted about the process by the Adoption Authority. If there's ongoing contact between the child and birth father adoption may not be considered the best option and in some cases shared guardianship is more appropriate. Irish law provides for consultation with children over the age of seven about the process.

The Adoption Authority of Ireland: www.aai.gov.ie.
Tel: 01 2309300.
Shelbourne House, Shelbourne Road, Dublin 4.

❋ ❋ ❋

leanne

path to freedom

Leanne[*] was a wild child who couldn't settle in school. She became pregnant as a teenager and went to live abroad. When she came back to Dublin she managed to build a good life for herself and her child.

Unfortunately Leanne allowed herself to drift into an abusive controlling relationship with Ian. She had a child with him and it took a long time and a lot of effort before she was able to end the relationship. She is now happy on her own and feels she is a successful parent and has a good relationship with both her children.

I was an out-of-control teenager. I came across as bubbly and flamboyant. My public persona was always upbeat, but underneath that I was very troubled. I couldn't understand why I wasn't able to concentrate. I didn't fit in or submit to discipline in school like my siblings and friends. I couldn't sit still or pay attention for very long. I didn't do very well academically and failed everything except home economics. The one thing I was amazing at was cooking.

I was a very popular kid even though I wasn't achieving. I had a great imagination and I liked people – I can honestly say that I've never met a stranger. I generally feel really good towards everyone and have always had lots of people I

[*] Names, occupations, locations and other identifying details have been altered to protect identities

consider to be close to me. I have a genuine love for people and I don't question their background, what they're doing or where they're at – I take them at face value.

When I was young there were no labels for me. In those days it wasn't normal to go to an educational psychologist or to be diagnosed as having attention deficit hyperactivity disorder (ADHD). So I ended up failing all my exams, leaving school early and doing a FÁS course in cooking. When I was sixteen I started working in catering.

The most important event in my life occurred when I got pregnant at seventeen. It affected me hugely. I realised immediately that I wouldn't be able to keep sucking my thumb and behaving like a child if I wanted to be a good mother.

I didn't tell my boyfriend, Timmy, I was pregnant. I thought that since he was sleeping with me that he should be aware of the possibility. I said to myself, 'If he doesn't ask me I'm not telling him,' and he didn't find out about Hannah until she was a toddler.

I felt awkward about getting pregnant and knew it wasn't going to go down well with my family, so I decided to go somewhere less conservative where I could enjoy my pregnancy without feeling self-conscious or ashamed of it.

I was just a kid when I jumped on a train and ended up in Amsterdam with no money and no job. The first thing I did when I arrived was buy batteries for my Walkman, as being able to listen to music was my priority! At seventeen your brain isn't fully developed and I didn't have a clue what I was doing.

I wasn't eligible for housing assistance or social welfare in the Netherlands, but people looked after me. I lived in rough areas, in houses that were abandoned and colonised by people from all over the world who had problems or were in trouble. I eventually ended up living in a nicer block of flats with a load of students. I had my own place in the block and the students thought I was great and rebellious, so everyone looked after me.

I went to see the local university doctor about my pregnancy and he was not impressed with me. He wouldn't look after me because he said I was living in an unsuitable area full of criminals. I didn't care about the broken windows – I thought my flat was a palace. I was conscious that I was living on the edge and didn't have a safety net but I loved being away from Dublin and I wasn't worried about the birth.

I didn't know what to expect when I went into labour. When my waters broke I actually thought I'd peed myself! I eventually figured out what was happening and got scared and called an ambulance. When I got into the ambulance I decided I didn't want to go to the hospital but the medics said, 'No, you can't get out,' so I had to go.

My labour wasn't nice at all. It was very long and I didn't have an epidural – I had pethidine and gas, which made me feel like a junkie. I thought to myself, 'Oh no, I've taken drugs; I don't know where I am.' I was scared I'd end up a drug addict afterwards.

Hannah was born during the summer and when I went back to my flat all my student friends had gone away. The first few weeks were funny. I was fine because I was breastfeeding and on cloud nine. I was delighted with Hannah: she was perfect and I doted on her. I'd nothing else to do except look after her. My family was keeping in touch with me but they were annoyed that I'd gone away, so there was some bad feeling between my parents and me.

When Hannah was nine months old I brought her home to Ireland. That was a big mistake. I thought I'd drawn a line in the sand and I was now an adult who was going to focus on her career and being a good mother, but my parents didn't see me that way.

I quickly got a job working as a junior chef in a restaurant. Then I had a real stroke of luck because the chef who hired me was suddenly fired by the owner of the restaurant. The owner was in big trouble because he needed someone to take over immediately. I went in to the owner and said, 'I'm a mother and I need to support myself. I need enough money to get my own place and look after my child, so please give me the job.' He knew I was serious so he gave me the job as head chef. I was only twenty.

Hannah was privately minded by a woman who took a couple of kids into her house, and things weren't too expensive in Dublin back then. I wasn't having a bad life; I was really busy but it was manageable. One day I met a friend of Hannah's dad by chance and she saw Hannah and put two and two together, so Timmy came back into our lives.

I met up with Timmy in a park and pointed to Hannah and said, 'She's yours.' Timmy was astonished. He was only twenty-one and it was the last thing he was expecting. We dated for a little while because it seemed right to try because of Hannah, but we never worked out as a couple and he had some difficult issues to deal with himself. Timmy sees Hannah from time to time now and they get on fine. There's no aggro in their relationship but they're not hugely close either.

My job paid well and with the help of my father I managed to get a mortgage to buy an apartment. This was a real achievement as a single working mother. It was during the 1980s, so property prices were still low and I was dying to buy somewhere so I wouldn't have to live at home and would have some independence. I bought an apartment in the city centre but it wasn't what I wanted. I would have preferred to live in a little cottage in the country, but it was handier to have an apartment when I was living and working in Dublin.

Things got difficult for me when the restaurant shut down. For a while I was a bit stuck. I got a job in another restaurant but it was stressful because it had a very late night shift and long hours. I was terrified I wasn't going to be able to pay my mortgage and I needed a live-in babysitter to look after Hannah during the night shift so things were hard for me.

Over the years I'd got to know lots of people in the restaurant business and it was through them that I met Ian. Ian was a very experienced chef. I won't say I fell in love with him but I looked up to him and I thought he was wise. He was ten years older than me and had children from a previous relationship. It seemed fair to me that we'd take on each other's children. Things were a bit weird in our relationship from the beginning but I didn't want to see that at the time.

Ian wasn't an ordinary person. If we were out socially he could be rude, arrogant and inappropriate towards women. He was overly chauvinistic and this didn't go down well in a group. I didn't want to see that aspect of him and I convinced myself that he wasn't really like that and that others were wrong about him. He made me feel safe because he told me that he'd help with the mortgage if I lost my job. I thought, 'OK, it's really nice to hear that.' I felt I could relax a bit and take chances that I mightn't normally take.

Ian encouraged me to give up my job and work with him on a freelance basis, doing catering for parties. This went really well for a while and it looked as if we were going to have a thriving, successful business together.

Hannah and I had a better quality of life with Ian. We drove around in a car instead of going everywhere on our bikes. We were able to go to the countryside, to Wicklow, for walks whenever we wanted to. Ian was an intelligent man and I enjoyed his company. And he was being nice to Hannah. That was very important to me and I would never have accepted anything less.

Ian knew what he was doing with the business and I suppose he was like a mentor to me. He made all the decisions in the catering company and that was fine with me at the time. He was older and more experienced.

I don't think I realised it then, but I had very quickly become remarkably submissive to Ian. I had lost my independence and started to do what he thought was right. He dismissed my opinions and criticised me a lot - that made me feel unlovable and vulnerable. I think Hannah was aware that something was wrong. She couldn't express it because she was young, but she made comments about me being quieter and Ian being bossy. I think she saw the change in me and sensed that Ian wasn't good for me.

After about a year we moved in together. I sold my flat

and we put the money from the sale and some of his money into a coffee shop. We lived over the shop and worked there all the time. Right away there were problems. We were arguing a lot about how to run the business. Ian was becoming more controlling and wouldn't let me hire people or deal with suppliers. He was rude and dismissive of me in front of customers and this led to a lot of arguments outside working hours.

Shortly after we bought the shop Ian said over breakfast one morning, 'I'm leaving,' and he walked out on me. He never said why. I was devastated. I didn't see him or know where he was for a week.

I know now that he was setting me up to see if I would put up with being in an abusive relationship. He was testing the boundaries to see how much I would take from him. I just felt stupid and had no insight into what was going on. I made all kinds of excuses for him. I thought he had commitment issues.

Ian used to drink a bit every single night, but I didn't see it as anything more than social drinking, as he didn't drink a huge amount on any one occasion. I know now that it was a problem because the alcohol gave him the Dutch courage he needed to be rude to me and to other people.

One week after Ian moved out he came back again, and we immediately got back together. He never explained why he'd left and I never asked. He then suggested that I stop taking the pill and I agreed because I didn't want him to leave again. I thought back then that we had a lot to offer each other and I was frightened of being on my own. I was wrong and I was frightened of the wrong thing.

I went off the pill and within two months I was pregnant.

I was delighted. The pregnancy wasn't as bad as my first. I was in a relationship and I had somewhere to live. I told my family I was doing it properly this time. I was organised and I had a man to share my life with.

After Ben was born I decided I wanted to do everything myself and didn't send him to a crèche or get a child minder. I wanted to enjoy the first two years of his life. Ian got his sister to help with our coffee shop and I spent all my time with the children.

Ian was useless with Ben when he was a baby. He wasn't unkind; he just didn't know how to look after him and wasn't tuned in to his needs. I tried to continue to have an input into the business but he wouldn't listen to anything I said. I wasn't happy with how he was running the coffee shop and felt that we should change some of our suppliers. He slated every suggestion I made and said I couldn't do anything right. At this point he had stopped doing the cooking and was instead serving the customers. He was so rude that he drove people away. I eventually managed to hire someone else to do the serving and things got back to normal.

I was living in a bubble with Ian and became allergic to the idea of being on my own. The situation sneaked up on me and there was a huge amount of denial on my part. I think living like that is a creative process. A lot of women who are in bad relationships with men create excuses and make allowances for them. You say to yourself, 'I have problems, he has problems, so when you add it up it's OK.' You start to think that you are equally as difficult as your partner. It's very difficult to get out of a relationship like that. You have to upset your entire life. Making excuses for your partner lets you off the hook and absolves you of the responsibility to do something about it.

An abusive person needs a submissive partner and there's a huge amount of psychology involved in how they set up their victim. They help you to create this situation in which you appear to be on the same level as them. But they will make sure that your self-esteem is lower than theirs and this is what creates your vulnerability. You recognise what they're doing on a subconscious level because it's a familiar role that you've already played in your life and you continue to play that role unconsciously. Even though deep down you know it's wrong you're too weak to do anything about it. You lack the motivation to end the relationship because your self-esteem and confidence are so low. The abuser can only feel that he's managing if he pushes your life into the basement. Mine was underground.

This went on for years and got worse and worse, it was a gradual decline. I ended up in a very low place. I eventually recognised that I was depressed when I got to a stage where I wasn't able to organise anything.

Ian had taken charge of everything to do with our lives at that time. I wasn't coping so he made an appointment for me to go to see a psychiatrist. I felt that the psychiatrist did very little to understand or analyse the causes of my depression, and instead he just prescribed me medication.

I took anti-depressants for a while but I didn't like them. It was as if I was taking a holiday from real life by being on the tablets. I slightly lost touch with reality and I started to feel numb, removed and disconnected from life. I caught sight of myself in a mirror in a shopping centre one day with my mouth gaping, and I realised that I was not participating in life or dealing with my problems by taking pills. It was just a way of covering it up.

I was OK coming off the anti-depressants, I accepted the side effects as I believed that my natural state was to be overemotional and tearful. The anti-depressants had made me lose touch with myself and I preferred to feel my real emotions rather than no emotions, even though they were painful. Both my children understood that I had moments when I couldn't cope and I don't think my parenting suffered because of my illness. I didn't ever call them into question. I'd say to them, 'I'm sorry I can't think straight today.' They understood that there was something in me that was causing the problem and that it was nothing to do with them. I was able to make it up to them when I felt better by doing things that were special, creative and fun.

My relationship with Ian was getting worse and worse and he had started directing nasty comments at my children. On one occasion he criticised Ben's ability at sports and I freaked out. Something clicked when he came out with a line that annihilated Ben and was clearly designed to undermine his confidence. I was at the end of my tether and there was no way I was going to allow him to do that to my child.

I confronted Ian about it and he reacted very aggressively. He wouldn't accept any criticism and he simply ignored me. He organised marriage counselling and I went to a few appointments with him. It was awful. He took over the sessions and I didn't say anything. He was very rude to me in front of the counsellor and said that all the problems in our relationship were my fault. If the counsellor tried to ask Ian any difficult questions he was quite aggressive when he answered.

He didn't turn up to the third appointment and I asked the counsellor what we should do and he said that he thought we should both get solicitors. I asked him if he was sure and he said, 'Get out of that relationship.' I was totally floored but I knew he was right.

There was a lot of anger and danger around this time. The abuse from Ian had gone from being emotional to physical and I feared for my life. He was getting drunk, being abusive and leaving a trail of destruction. I called the gardaí and told them that if he came near me I'd kill him out of fear of having to deal with him and to protect my children. It came to a physical battle to get him to leave the house. He didn't want to go but I felt it was the children's home and there was no way I was leaving him alone with them.

The physical abuse was the last straw and I needed to protect my children – a mother's instinct is stronger than anything. I think the advice the counsellor had given me to get out of the relationship had sunk in. I had to get out because the relationship had gone from being difficult to impossible. I felt deep fear for my children and it woke me up. I began to realise that I wasn't the one who had caused the problems.

Ian and I fought over the house and the shop and eventually I locked him out. He moved out and then he came back and took the car. I didn't care – I just wanted him out.

When I heard his voice after that I finally realised that I didn't trust him. It was like a massive coin had dropped. It was the voice that I'd listened to for ten years and I knew that he had never been the man I thought he was.

I got a solicitor and when I discussed it with him

he reacted with huge sympathy and said I was in a very dangerous situation. He told me I had to take action and that the law was on my side and I needed to sort out my kids, my financial situation and have Ian barred from the house.

I now felt that I could be open about the truth of my situation because I was going to court and discussing my case with family and friends. People were able to say to me: 'Look at what he's done to you.' It was like the curtains had come back from a big movie screen and I was finally able to see the big picture.

It took me a long time to identify our problems. The understanding I gained helped me to accept myself and change my life. I felt lighter because I was taking the bull by the horns. I think it was important for my children to see me being strong. If they had continued to witness Ian's inhumane behaviour, then the pattern might have repeated itself for them. What you grow up with gives you a manual of how to live and I didn't want them to grow up with the wrong manual.

I knew my children weren't going to emerge from this unscathed but I was not going to allow it to destroy them. I have had a great relationship with my children from day one and that is unbreakable. There was no question in my mind as to who was being the bad parent.

My solicitor was a friend of a friend and that made things easier for me. I felt that I was getting some compassion along with the information. This helped as I was very nervous and confused about the whole thing.

I thought it would take about six months to sort out the property and the business. I had put money into it from the sale of my apartment so I didn't see how I could lose. I had two children and I had the power and the strength to believe in my cause. There was no way I was going to lose the roof over our heads.

The solicitor explained to me that it would take much longer than six months and from what he understood about Ian he would drag it out for as long as he possibly could. He told me: 'This guy is going to take you for the whole nine yards,' and he was right. Ian didn't make anything easy for me. That was a shock as I thought he would put the children first. In the end it took five years to resolve. It was awkward because we weren't married, so it was hard to explain that we were a family unit. The legal people were talking about property, business and partition. I didn't want to know about any of that, as I was a mother in an awful predicament and my main concern was sorting out the issues surrounding the children. The legal people didn't see it that way.

My barrister bent the rules a bit when she drafted the proceedings. She made sure that my case ended up in the family courts. It was worth the risk because while it was in the family courts the whole truth of the situation came out. All the issues were aired together: maintenance, access and guardianship were put in with the property issues. This wasn't quite following the letter of the law because we weren't married, but it worked well.

Both Ian and I had to see psychologists, which helped my case a lot because it confirmed my suspicions that he had a personality disorder. My children were lucky. It took a long time for the case to get to court and during that time they grew up and moved on from the problems they experienced with Ian. Ian wanted to have access to Ben but he didn't keep his appointments with the psychologist, so this was denied.

The psychologist was appalled by his attitude. He refused to accept that he had done anything wrong. He shouted and argued with her during the session, I think he scared her and he wouldn't answer her questions. He claimed that I had provoked him to violence and she didn't believe him so her report was really damning.

The gardaí were excellent. A female garda rang me out of the blue one day and said to me: 'I was thinking of you, how are you getting along?' I never expected that kindness from the police and I was really amazed. Another day I was at one of our many court appearances and she asked me if was I there on my own. I said yes and she said, 'You're not now,' and sat down beside me.

My father told me that Ian was a coward and a taker and that I had to stand up to him and that would do it. I think that if he wasn't so cowardly he'd be dangerous. He needs a warning label for other women. He's unable to have a relationship with anyone and was never in love with me. I was just an opportunity for him.

I got huge support from everyone. People were more than helpful. Marriage counsellors, psychologists, solicitors, barristers, gardaí – they were all there when I needed them.

I was very confused for the first couple of years while things were going through the system. It's normal to be like that after years of emotional abuse but people don't understand it because it can't be seen or photographed. It's hard to explain how it happens, how it leaves you feeling and how long it takes to pull yourself back from it.

The guardianship and access part of our court case took ages. I realised that access was the most important issue. Ben didn't want to see Ian but he kept applying for access and was refused three times. Each time he applied, the psychologist's report was pulled out and he was refused, so I didn't have to give evidence.

My other concern was what was going to happen to our business and the property. Ian said for years that he'd let me buy him out but every time my solicitor tried to negotiate, he would give him the run-around. He was very uncooperative and it became clearer and clearer that he wasn't going to give in. I couldn't understand why he would want to turn his child out of his home.

It was five years before we finally went to court over the property and I was highly anxious about what was going to happen. I had to give evidence at the hearing. My dad was great. He gave evidence that he'd given us money towards the business and that I had sold my apartment as well, so it was obvious that Ian hadn't contributed much. He was aggressive in court and it was clear that he wasn't going to bend for anyone.

It was a very gripping moment in court because I was hoping the judge wasn't going to divide the property and the business physically so we'd have to share it as neighbours. I knew there was no way that could work and Ian would have been over the moon to have me back under his thumb.

The judge saw that Ian was being unrealistic and unreasonable and we were allowed to buy him out of his share of the property and the business. He was ordered to pay a small amount of maintenance for Ben every month. He does pay this and I always tell Ben when it arrives because it's important to give credit where it's due.

I've said to Ben that it's up to him if he wants to have any contact with Ian. There is the odd phone call and Ian is less aggressive now. I don't have to be there beside Ben when he's on the phone any more, as I'm not so worried about what he's going to say. I know that Ben is still scared of Ian and doesn't want to see him. He said to me: 'Mum, why would I want to upset my life by seeing him? I'm happy.' I always tell him that he doesn't have to follow my opinion and that he can have his own opinion. I wouldn't press him to make up his mind. Every few months I say to him: 'You might feel differently one day, so you must do your own thing and whatever you decide to do I will be supportive.'

It broke my heart that Ian left Ben in such a quandary. He was under a lot of pressure and I feel he had no choice but to slot in with me. I don't think it's fair that he didn't have a choice but it had to be like that. In a normal family a kid can bounce off both parents. We're in a minus situation and it's very difficult. If Ian had died it would have been easier – you can't argue with death. You can drive yourself crazy trying to ponder the morality of what happened but I have no doubt that I did the right thing.

I asked Ben when he was about ten if he wanted to have a punch bag. I thought it would be good for him to have something on which he could take out any aggression he was feeling. I've always made sure that he has the freedom to express his feelings of anger and sadness. While everything was happening Ben used to say to me, 'Mum, there's one thing that I want and that is not to have to move away from my school or my friends.' I said to myself, 'Right, that's top of the list.' I felt I was suddenly pushed into having to make lots and lots of decisions on my own and when Ben had input it was really helpful. I wanted him to know that he was a huge priority in my life.

We stayed living above the coffee shop and it was difficult. A lot of people around the area knew what had happened and it would have been easier for me to move away to a place where the whole community didn't know my business. But at the same time I think it was great that Ben made the decision that we would stay because that fixed our future, and, at the end of the day, the friendships he has have become more important to him than they might otherwise have been. I've spent an awful lot of time and energy on homemaking and creating an environment that's happy and secure for Ben.

Because there's a big age gap between Ben and Hannah I've been able to deal with the children one at a time. Hannah was much less affected by the break-up than Ben because of her age and because of the fact that she's very independent and has her own interests and lots of great friends. She works with me in the shop and she does a brilliant job. If she wants to do something else in the future I'll support her all the way.

Since Ian has left, the atmosphere in the house has improved beyond my greatest expectations. We lived with oppression for so long that the liberation was turbulent too. There was intense upset and we've all laughed and cried because now everyone has the space to express themselves.

After the final court date I was delighted. What I thought and believed should happen did happen and I felt vindicated. I reclaimed the confidence I'd lost and was given a new chance to move on.

I was afraid for a while that Ian might appeal the decision but even if he had it wouldn't have been so bad. I think we had been through the worst of it. We had somewhere to live and I had my business, so we quietly celebrated the fact that we didn't have to worry any more about where to live or what the future held.

I've finally found that I'm happy as a single person. That's a huge achievement for me and it's taken a long, long time. The parenting has got easier as my children have got older and Ben has no issues.

My situation was difficult legally because I wasn't married. I think it's great that there are new laws now that give some protection to unmarried parents. It's hard to get justice unless the courts can see your case in the context of your family problems rather than as a dispute over a business. I was lucky that my barrister was able to organise things so my case was heard in the family courts. I was also very lucky that the judge understood everything I'd been through. I'm happy now and very optimistic about our future.

❋ ❋ ❋

Women's Aid

Women's Aid is a national organisation that works to address the issue of domestic violence in Ireland. It is a feminist, political and campaigning organisation that is committed to the elimination of violence and abuse.

Women's Aid provides help and information for women who are experiencing domestic violence through its support lines and support centres. It provides a court accompaniment service and refers women to local domestic violence support services and refuges.

The organisation describes some of the warning signs of an abusive relationship as follows:

- *You are afraid of your partner*
- *You are constantly walking on eggshells because of his mood swings*
- *He loses his temper easily over minor things*
- *He has hit you or almost hit you and/or your children*
- *He calls you names and threatens you and/or your children*
- *He regularly criticises you or undermines you in front of other people*
- *He has threatened to have you deported because of your immigration status*
- *He tries to control aspects of your life such as where you work, who you see, what you spend and what you wear*

Women's Aid: www.womensaid.ie
Freephone helpline: 1800 341 900
(Monday – Sunday 10 a.m. to 10 p.m.)

❋ ❋ ❋

oisín

keep the devil from your door

Oisín[*] is a creative, artistic man. He had a slow start to his career as a writer but he became a successful editor later in life. He met Suzanne when they were young and they worked together as publishers and had two children.

Suzanne met Carlos in Spain when the children were young and immediately ended her marriage and went to live with him. Oisín was shocked at how quickly their marriage unravelled.

He negotiated a separation agreement with Suzanne and they lived near to each other and shared custody of the children. Oisín found the process difficult but didn't allow himself to become bitter or consumed by a desire for revenge.

I grew up in the suburbs of Dublin and went to a Christian Brothers junior school. At the time it was a very homogenous, all-boys school run by religious brothers. I hated it – it was a strict and repressed environment. I had some older siblings and I got on very well with everyone in my family. We had a relatively comfortable upbringing. When I hear people talking

[*] Names, occupations, locations and other identifying details have been altered to protect identities

about the negative things that went on in their families when they were growing up, I can't relate to them.

When the time came to go to secondary school, my parents decided to send me to a new, progressive comprehensive school. I think it was set up for Protestants and people from other backgrounds so they would be able to access a free school. It was non-denominational and had a liberal atmosphere. It was big culture shock to move there from a Christian Brothers school. I had come from an all-boys environment, where everyone had Irish names and everyone was the same, to this amazing place. I loved it there.

Suddenly I was in the company of two alien beings – Protestants and girls. It was great. My class was full of extraordinarily pretty girls. They were all beautiful in my young eyes. They had exotic names like Ingrid and Wendy. In my old world the girls were called Mary and Teresa. I felt a weird divide between them and me. I had this strange impression that they were illicit, foreign and British – the enemy. There were also other foreign girls in my class, who were half Chinese or from other European countries.

I didn't have any girlfriends while I was in school but I did have crushes on girls the whole way through. I think my year was a particularly pretty year and I still reminisce. There were girls in the class who were interested in me but I was too shy at that stage to ask them out.

After I did the Leaving Cert I went away travelling for a year. When I came back to Dublin, I decided I was going to be a writer. I tried writing for four years and realised that I wasn't getting anywhere. I was in my twenties and I hadn't made a penny. I tried to think of something that was more straight-laced, so I thought I would become a journalist. I found a course I was interested in doing and I went back to college. I found the course great but it was a compromise as far as I was concerned. I was quite artistic and a bit flaky, but over time I got interested in journalism and became hooked on writing for newspapers and magazines.

I met Suzanne when I was very young. She was in the class below me in school and I was quite keen on her then. She was in my social circle for years and I knew all her friends and she knew mine. She was having an on-off relationship with a friend of a friend, so I would see her occasionally at parties or in pubs.

Some friends set us up when Suzanne was single and we all met up at a music festival. I was twenty-one and she was twenty. We got on very well and started going out and never looked back. Two years later we began living together in a cool flat in town. She had studied English and was working in publishing so we were both doing the same thing from different angles and we had lots in common.

We moved to London for a while and worked in magazines and newspapers. She ended up getting into the marketing end of it and I was editing. We bought a house in London and were thinking of settling there. On a trip back to Dublin an opportunity arose for us both to get involved in setting up a new publication in Ireland, so we decided to sell our place in London and move back home.

We rented a nice place in the city centre for a few years and worked really hard setting up the new magazine. We decided to get married as we'd been together for eight years and it seemed like the right thing to do. Our son was born two years later.

Nothing changed in our lives or our relationship for a long time. Everything was fine for years. We were both extremely focused on our careers and on making the magazine a success. It was a big adventure. We were responsible for everything: getting advertising, hiring and firing, and writing stories. It was an amazing time.

We were renting a flat very near to where we worked and we had a great woman who lived nearby minding our son. She didn't mind taking him late in the evenings or overnight if we needed help. If we were stuck we were able to work at home or bring him into the office. Childminding was never a problem.

Then we decided to have another child. Our daughter was born three years after our son and suddenly everything got very difficult. We were working hard and were out a lot in the evenings and we were having problems getting a minder for two children. The logistics were becoming impossible. Our flat was very small and we knew we needed somewhere bigger and live-in help. We had this idea that it would be nice for the kids if we lived by the sea, so we decided to buy a house with a garden out in Malahide. There was a great crèche nearby and plenty of schools.

Our daughter was colicky when she was a baby. She didn't sleep at all and it was hell. We ended up all sleeping in the bed together for about a year. There is an animalistic beauty to that, but it was no fun trying to work without any sleep and not knowing when we would get any sleep. You have to do it and you know it will stop eventually, but it is hard.

Despite the problems, I don't think that time affected our relationship too much. We kept working and Suzanne and I were given an opportunity to get involved in starting up another publication. We thought the idea was great and decided that we'd put our savings into it. Getting the publication started was very difficult and we ended up putting ourselves under huge financial strain. Our expenses were mounting. We had to pay the mortgage and a huge amount for childcare, and everything was getting more and more expensive.

We had bought a house that was expensive and I was beginning to regret the move. I don't know why we were so obsessed with owning our own house. I don't think we actually needed it. I think you can just get locked into ideas of what you should be doing and that's what everyone in Ireland was doing at the time. Also, Malahide was too far from town for us. If we wanted to go out for a night we had to get babysitters and taxis, and by the time we'd paid for drinks and dinner we could have gone to London for the weekend for the same amount of money. At the time there was a lot of pressure on people to be having a good time and I suppose we fell into that trap.

Things got very difficult with the magazine. We couldn't get the advertising revenue we needed. We believed that once we'd got the things up and running we'd get a huge readership, but the first year was hell. When I look back at that time it was like being in a boxing ring and fighting for our lives.

It was insane, but it was completely self-inflicted. We didn't have to invest in the magazine, but we really believed in it. It was what we did and part of our identity. No one could advise us what to do because we were determined to make it work. We weren't going to walk away from it. We ended up arguing a lot about the direction the magazine should take. It was a bad time for us as a couple.

After three years the magazine was beginning to break even. But the stress of getting it to that stage had taken its toll on us. I wanted to sell it just to get rid of it. I felt a responsibility to the people who worked there but I didn't want to run it any more. There were some larger publications interested in taking it on, so I started negotiating with them.

We weren't able to run the magazine efficiently ourselves. It was a great publication but it needed an owner with deep pockets and management experience. There was a litany of disasters. Everything that could have gone wrong went wrong. We had legal problems, problems with staff and problems with advertisers. Each problem was more horrendous than the last. After all the work we had put in, it was hard to give up on it. I think we were both too in love with the magazine to be sensible and walk away when it wasn't working.

We were getting to the stage where we were going to be able to sell up for a little money and walk away. I was relieved and happy but Suzanne wasn't. Then, out of the blue, I got offered a really good, well-paid job editing a prestigious publication. I was delighted. I didn't want to go through starting up another magazine and I felt it was an opportunity for us as a family to get some breathing space.

It was a three-year contract and we discussed it as a family. I didn't jump in and take it without getting Suzanne's opinion. Eventually, we decided that I should take the job. I think this was very difficult for Suzanne. The magazine was like her third child and she cared deeply about it. When we sold it, she wasn't asked to stay on as a consultant, so she was out of a job. I think she felt pissed off and resentful that I was working and she wasn't.

Suzanne is the kind of woman who definitely needs a career. She is wired to have children but she's also driven and likes to work hard. In her mind there's no recognition for having kids. She didn't love the whole mummy thing of being sociable with other mothers at the school gate. Parenting is a long haul for everyone and it was important to her, but it didn't define her.

Eventually Suzanne got some freelance work as a travel writer. Most of it was in Ireland but some of it was abroad. She was travelling around Europe and I was happy that she had something to do.

She went to a press weekend for a new hotel one weekend and she met a Spanish journalist there. And that was it. I didn't know what had happened but I suddenly felt that something was terribly wrong. I sat down with her and asked her, 'What's the story?' She was very troubled and I knew her behaviour was odd. I thought, 'Oh fuck, are we actually breaking up?'

Then we had this long process where Suzanne was making up her mind what to do. We had been together eight years before we'd got married and we'd been married for twelve years. We had a son and a daughter together. It was such a tough thing to go through.

The whole thing was horrible. Normally you'd expect things to end gradually. This was so sudden. We hadn't stopped having sex; we hadn't been arguing more than normal; we weren't estranged; we were still talking. I didn't believe it was actually happening. I couldn't connect reality with the circumstances.

Then she told me, 'This is it. This is the plan. I'm leaving.' I was devastated and was left in total shock. I had no idea she would actually do that and leave me with the children. I couldn't understand it. If Martians had landed in the front garden I would have been less surprised. I was so low after she left that I don't think I ate anything for months.

We had an au pair booked to come and help out, so that distracted me a bit. I felt awkward about having a girl come to live in the house when I was living on my own with the children, but it worked out OK and she was a great help in the beginning.

Suzanne moved out and went to live in Spain for a year. She was so completely in love with this Spanish guy that she was able to walk out on the children and me. I was so upset that I didn't do or say anything for ages. I didn't tell my family or friends because I couldn't put what had happened into words. I couldn't start to give an account of what had happened.

I vacillated between thinking, 'Should I shoot myself? Get a shotgun and kill myself?' and thinking, 'Should I shoot them?' I was so scared about what was going to happen to me in the end. Was I going to end up homeless and only being able to see my children at weekends? You hear such horrible stories. I didn't know how things were going to work out and I was frightened.

Suzanne was determined that there was going to be no mediation or counselling. I went to a mediator to discuss the situation on my own and he said to me, 'You do know it takes two to tango? This is clearly over, so what are you going to do next?' My wife was sure that this was the way it was going to be and there was no way I could change her mind.

The one thing I can't forgive is how she told the children. They were only ten and eight. She decided that she wanted to discuss the break-up with them as soon as it happened. I didn't want to. I thought it would be best to see how things went and see if we could tell them in six months or so. I was hoping that maybe she'd see some sense and come back to us. She went ahead and told them. I've never seen them so upset; they cried their eyes out.

Suzanne told me that she wanted to take the kids with her to Spain to meet her new partner. I said to her, 'Will you please wait?' She said, 'Absolutely not.' So she took them over to meet him. I thought maybe it would end and he might dump her after a year, so I really didn't want my children to meet him.

I never spoke to my kids about any of this – I just didn't know how to. I don't think it would have been helpful. I didn't ask them how it went when they went over to Spain to meet Carlos because I didn't want to know. The kids seemed to get on well with him when they went over and they were fine.

I spent all my time trying not to get into a big row with Suzanne. The desire for revenge is huge and, inevitably, completely destructive, so I focused on protecting my children. My idea of what was going to happen was that the children were going to stay with me. I told her that this was the family home and that it was going to be their anchor and their stability. I think she wanted to take the kids to Spain but she knew she couldn't take them away from their home to a different country with a different language.

Suzanne tried living in Spain for a while, coming back and forth to see the children, and bringing them over to see her, but it didn't work. They were too young and it was difficult getting them over there and back to Ireland again. She realised it was a big production. After a year she and Carlos moved to Ireland. I was relieved and worried at the same time. I don't know how Carlos sorted out his work situation; I never asked. Maybe he travelled back and forth to Spain. I really don't know. They bought a small house in Dublin, so they weren't loaded.

I got in touch with one of my best friends a few months after Suzanne left. He had been through a separation and a divorce and I needed to talk to someone. I told him on the phone what was going on and he dropped everything he was doing and came to see me. He took me out to dinner and gave me lots of advice. He gave me the telephone number of a barrister who was a friend of his and I called her. It was great to get support because at that point I was completely at sea. I was dreading the idea of legal proceedings, going to court, having to give evidence and all the hassle.

I spoke to the barrister and she introduced me to a solicitor and we all got together for a meeting. They were both really good and very supportive. They said to me that they thought I should try to avoid confrontation. The solicitor said that we could write an attack letter and kick things off but that it might be better to let the situation unfold and see what happens. In hindsight I think that was good advice. I suspect that when you attack your ex in this type of situation, you get attacked back.

Suzanne had her own solicitor and he wanted to take a more confrontational approach to everything. Obviously lawyers are trained to do that and he was doing his job. He told Suzanne that she shouldn't move out of the family home. It was too late to advise her on that because there was no way she could move back in after living with Carlos. If she wanted to maximise her position then she had played it completely wrong.

Suzanne had a friend who was going through an incredibly acrimonious divorce at the time and she saw what it was like first hand. I think that made her realise that it was not the way to go. She knew from work what legal bills could be like and she wasn't going to go there. She didn't want all the money to go to the lawyers.

My costs worked out fine. I only had to pay for the time I had with my solicitor and the costs for drafting the separation agreement. It wasn't an arm and a leg. I know from talking to friends that if it goes to court and you fight all the way, it can cost tens of thousands.

Disassembling our lives together was a nightmare because everything we had was in joint names. I negotiated with Suzanne and we talked it out over the year. It was difficult. When it comes to money, everyone wants to improve his or her position. I suggested a scenario that I thought was fair. I gave Suzanne a figure of what I could afford to buy her out. She was very anxious to sell the house but I felt that the level of disruption would be too much for the children.

It took a lot of to-ing and fro-ing and it was a year before we had a signed agreement. She eventually agreed to let me buy her out. That year seemed like forever to me. I think I was in a stronger position than her when it came to negotiating because she was under pressure to get some money so she could buy a place to live in Dublin. If we had gone to court it might have taken years to work things out.

Just after we settled everything, Suzanne and Carlos moved into a house near to where I lived. It was only a few streets away and in terms of the management of the family it was great. If the kids forgot something or needed toys or schoolbooks, they could walk back to the house to get them. They were always within walking distance of school and it gave them great stability.

At the same time, I wasn't exactly thrilled to have Suzanne and Carlos living so near to me. I didn't walk down their street very often. She never asked me how I felt about it, and I did see Carlos on the street a few times. I found that difficult, but I couldn't do anything about it.

We decided that we would share custody – one week on and one week off. It worked out fairly OK. There were moments of tension so I tried to avoid seeing Suzanne if I could. I had no sense that she wanted to see more of the children and it was fine by me that I had them half of the time. I was used to doing a lot of work at home and the children were old enough to be minded by an au pair. We also had some great babysitters from the area who looked after them when they were a bit older.

It was intense and busy when the kids were around and lonely for me when they were gone. They were fairly cool about it. When there were parent-teacher meetings or events that we had to go to together as parents, I went with Suzanne and didn't make a big deal about it.

I used to take the kids away on holidays and we had great adventures. They loved Key Camp holidays in France so we did lots of those and I have lovely memories of our summers together. We became very close during those times. The moody teen years were hellish but we got over them.

Of course there was gossip when Suzanne and I split up. You have to be prepared for that. All our friends knew about it – I couldn't keep it a secret. I think people did take sides. One or two friends tried to see both of us, but then drifted towards one or the other.

I don't think Suzanne was very happy with the agreement. She was moody and tricky to deal with afterwards. I got the impression for a while that she wanted to go back and renegotiate. She wrote to my solicitor once or twice, looking to revisit it, and my solicitor sent rebuttal letters back. I felt like there was a shadow hanging over things for a few years, even after we had made the agreement. I used to panic and worry that there might be something worse coming down the road. Then somehow it all went away and it never arose again. I think Suzanne made a decision that she wasn't going to go down that route.

I dated a bit when the kids were young. I used to keep it to the times when I was off duty. I didn't introduce the kids to any of my girlfriends until they were much older. I have a new partner now who lives with me. She's a writer as well and she's quite different from my ex. She's much more sociable; she's not moody and she's good fun.

I never sat down with the kids and asked, 'How do you feel about the break-up?' I was too angry. I'm never going to have any view except my own, which is that Suzanne is a bitch. I don't want to transfer those feelings onto my children. I don't think that would be a good thing to do. They can make up their own minds.

I think life was difficult for Suzanne and Carlos. They probably didn't have a lot of money. I didn't ask the children how things were going between them, but you can sense things. They lived together for four years and then I heard that he went back to Spain and Suzanne was living on her own. My daughter told me that they were breaking up because they didn't get on and that they used to have a lot of bitter arguments. I think she was crazy to ruin our marriage for an affair that only lasted a few years. If she had a different set of morals she could have hidden it from me and kept seeing him, without leaving me at all.

If it had been a brief affair and it had broken up earlier, maybe things would have been different. She was determined when she met Carlos to 'cut down the tree'. There was no way she was leaving a door open to work things out. Since then I've wanted nothing to do with her. She's moved house now and lives further away and I keep contact to a minimum.

It's hard to say why Suzanne did what she did. I think it might have to do with us getting together so young. I think she had a midlife crisis. She's not a regular woman. She's very focused on her career and that is part of who she is. Maybe after twenty years with me she said to herself, 'Is this all there is?' I was happy with our life and I thought if we had problems we could have improved things. We had a lot going for us as a family. I think she was intoxicated by her romance with Carlos and she must have thought it was going to last.

Suzanne's career went OK for her but it wasn't brilliant. I remember being on holidays one time and she rang me and ranted and raved about something she wanted me to do for her professionally. I didn't know what she was talking about and I didn't want to go there so I hung up the phone.

My kids are great. They don't do brilliantly academically

but I'm not worried about it. I only got myself together after school, so they can take their time. They have great ambitions but they don't study. I understand that because I can't say that I took things seriously when I was their age. They are having fun. I've said to them that I can't pay for the party indefinitely, so I'll start putting my foot down by degrees. I'm encouraging them to travel abroad too.

It took me a few years to get over the separation. It was like a death. I suppose in some ways you don't get over it at all. I worked on myself but I didn't do any counselling or anything like that. I'm not a therapy type person. I probably should go but it seems a bit indulgent – a bit new age or Californian.

I don't have any regrets about what I did or about how I handled things. After Suzanne and I signed the separation agreement I never thought we would get back together. I just kept on going with my life. The marriage didn't work, so I accepted that and it was onwards and upwards for me. I don't dwell on it.

There is evil in the desire for revenge and I'm glad I didn't go there. It's a destructive emotion and of no value. It's like letting the devil into your house.

❋ ❋ ❋

The Divorce Act 1996

When the court grants a divorce in Ireland, by law the judge must be satisfied that 'such provision as the court considers proper having regard to the circumstances exists or would be made for the spouses and any dependant members of the family'. Simply put, by law the court has to look at certain factors so that it can work out how each partner and their dependants should be provided for after a divorce is granted.

Those factors are set out in Section 20 of the Divorce Act and they are as follows:

- *The income, earning capacity, property and other financial resources of each spouse at the time or in the foreseeable future*
- *The financial needs, obligations and responsibilities of each spouse at the time or in the foreseeable future (whether in the case of remarriage or not)*
- *The standard of living enjoyed by the family before the proceedings began or the spouses started to live apart*
- *The age of the spouses, duration of marriage and length of time they lived together*
- *Any physical or mental disability of either spouse*
- *The contribution which each spouse has made (or is likely to make) to the welfare of the family, including contributions to the income, earning capacity, property and financial resources of the other spouse, and any contribution made by looking after the home or caring for the family*
- *The effect of marital responsibility on the earning capacity of either spouse while they were living together, and particularly the degree to which a spouse's future earning capacity was affected by giving up the possibility of paid work to look after the home or care for the family*
- *Any income or benefits to which either spouse is statutorily entitled*
- *The conduct of either of the spouses, if it would be unfair, in all the circumstances, to disregard such conduct*
- *The accommodation needs of either spouse*

- *The value to either spouse of any benefit (such as a pension) which would be lost because of the divorce*
- *The rights of anyone else, including a new husband or* wife

❋ ❋ ❋

eleanor

behind the mask

Eleanor[*] speaks like Audrey Hepburn. She's a petite, elegant, well-dressed lady, seemingly from another era. Her parents were English and she grew up with a very well-off, privileged background in the Irish countryside.

As a young adult she found it hard to commit to a direction for her life. She met and fell in love with Roger, who seemed like the perfect man.

After five years of marriage, Roger suddenly left her with their two children and no support. They separated and Eleanor was left to bring up the children on her own. She found it difficult being single in Dublin and worked hard to look after her children. She was happy to see them leave home and work abroad.

My parents were originally from England. They were very well off and were passionate about sailing, so I grew up in a large house by the sea with lots of land and boats. Both my parents were extremely well educated and my father was very successful.

I was the eldest in the family and had a very privileged upbringing. I was a bit spoilt and got on very well with my father. He was a driven perfectionist and expected a lot from me. I don't remember my mother having a huge input

---

* Names, occupations, locations and other identifying details have been altered to protect identities

when I was young. She wasn't that interested in me and she adored my brother.

We were from a Church of Ireland background and that meant that we were a bit isolated in Ireland. I was sent to boarding school at the age of nine. I didn't like it there very much. I wanted to be at home, out on my boat. I loved the land and the sea and couldn't stand being at school.

When I was fourteen I caused uproar at school and insisted that I be allowed to go home and go to a day school. My parents acquiesced and I spent the rest of my schooldays going to the local school and living at home.

My father was ambitious for me and he wanted me to do medicine or law. I didn't do too well in my exams so I ended up studying arts in Trinity. I didn't study very much and switched courses a few times. I was a bit of a mess academically.

In my late teens and early twenties I felt like I was living in a dense fog. I couldn't settle down and I was quite confused about what I was doing and didn't finish my degree. As I got older I travelled around but never stayed in the same country longer than a few months. I looked as if I was having fun but inside I was lost.

I was in an awful accident when I was twenty and I thought I'd never be able to sail again. I was on crutches for ages. My father encouraged me to go out on a trip before I was properly recovered and the boat capsized and I broke my arm. After that I lost my confidence completely and I could never sail again. I shouldn't really have been out that day.

In my twenties I felt I was failing my father by not being able to sail any more and by not finishing my education. I felt guilt for not fulfilling his ambitions for me. He was a fair man and a great man but when I didn't measure up I could feel him closing down. He was quite judgmental of me but he was ill towards the end of his life, so maybe it was his illness that made him like that.

I had no steady relationships with men when I was young. Nothing sticks out in my mind about that time. I think I was probably a bit 'man mad'. I know I was looking for security, as I didn't feel emotionally secure with my parents. I was lucky because they did give me financial security. My father was very generous and always supported me.

I studied and worked in Paris for a while and then I decided to come back to Dublin. My father lent me a flat back in Dublin to live in. I didn't realise how privileged I was when I was young – being given the use of an enormous flat at twenty-three. I shared the flat with a friend and went back to study. The teaching in my college was terrible and I couldn't do the coursework. I was quite artistic and liked to take photographs. I was quite a good photographer, but my father used to say, 'There are no artists in this family.'

I was twenty-five when I met my husband, Roger. My father had died a few months previously and I was hopping to and fro all over the place. I could pitch up in England and stay with relatives when I wanted to, and sometimes I'd drive off to Europe on a whim.

I met Roger in the South of France. I'd driven there with a friend. I was sitting outside a café and there he was. He was younger than me and had been born in France, but he lived in London. He had a very troubled background, with an unfaithful and useless father. No one knew his real history. His family were originally Eastern European but it was very unclear where exactly they were from. They might have been German or Polish. I know they changed their name. Roger grew up with his father's lies and deceptions about his involvement with various women and his father had several children with other women. Although Roger's family were educated, he didn't have any education himself.

I found Roger to be very kind. He was attentive and loving and made me feel totally secure. He was tall and I'm very small! I was a bit worried because he didn't have a job, but I thought he would get one at some stage, so it wasn't an issue.

We were living together in England and I was very happy. This was a bit unusual in those days; none of my friends lived with their boyfriends in Ireland and my family were furious. I had some money from my inheritance from my father that provided us with an income. I still had the use of the flat in Dublin when I was at home but at that time it was owned by my mother. I was working for an antiques dealer in London – it was a job I loved. We weren't able to live on the money we were earning without my family's money, but I saw that money as a help rather than the main source of income. I had ambitions for our future and I had a vague idea that we might start a business together.

While we were living in London, I got a phone call from home saying there were problems with aspects of my father's will that had to be discussed and would I please come home. I was worried about my inheritance and the flat, so I rushed home to my mother. As soon as I got back I realised it was all a ruse to get me away from Roger, as everyone thought he was unsuitable and had no prospects.

Roger followed me back to Dublin. I was happy

about that because I felt I couldn't live without him. I was passionately in love; he was the apple of my eye. We stayed in my mother's flat in Dublin and started an antiques exporting business together. We sourced antiques in Ireland and exported them to dealers in England.

If my father had been alive he would have hounded Roger out of the country. My mother wouldn't do that because she was quite a reserved person but, with hindsight, she was quite right to try to get me away from him.

Roger was such a charming man. He could charm the birds off the trees. Some people might have seen through him but most people just thought he was lovely. In the early years our antiques business was a bit rocky but we did some good deals and made some money and got established.

We lived and worked together in Dublin for three years and then we got married. We got married in a registry office, which was fine with our families because none of us are religious, and we had a party at home. My mother gave us a house to live in that was part of my father's estate and we still had the use of the flat in Dublin, as an office for our business. The house we lived in was in the country and it was fantastic. We had horses and other animals and it was an idyllic place for the children when they were young.

We were married for about five years and had two children together. I was happy and thought things were great. Roger was a bit hopeless around the house and it was always a mess when I came back from hospital after having the babies. He didn't help much and was always running off to work. But, in fairness, he was fantastic at getting up to feed them in the middle of the night and he was good at playing with them when they were small. When they were young I was looking after the children in the country and he was up and down to Dublin buying and selling antiques.

One morning Roger sat down in the kitchen after breakfast. The children were playing in the garden, and he said, 'I don't want to be married any more.'

I wasn't able to think. I said, 'Would you just hold on here and look after the children while I do the shopping.' I went off and did the shopping, and when I got back his bags were packed. I thought I'd lost my wedding ring that day but I found it in my room months later. I must have taken it off while I was in a trance.

I was numb for a few days and couldn't think, I think it was a chemical reaction to the shock. I didn't react in a normal way by crying or getting upset. My mind definitely stopped working and something else kept me going.

I had no idea what was going on or why Roger had left. About ten days later, somebody told me that Roger had a girlfriend and that she had a child. I still remember the thud in my stomach when I heard that. I remember exactly where I was sitting and who I was talking to. My whole world just blew up and it all dawned on me. He had being seeing someone else for a long time. I was in shock.

I went home to my mother's. I remember she was doing the gardening and I went straight up to her and said, 'I have to tell you that he has another child.' I disintegrated. My mother had to call the GP for me. It must have been awful for my mother to see her child in that state.

I found out that Roger's other child was only three months younger than my son. Then the shit really hit the fan. I talked to all my friends and discovered that he had been with a lot of different women. This was worse than him moving out. I felt every emotion under the sun. I was in a very bad way. My whole world had fallen apart and I couldn't handle it. I had a two-year-old and a four-year-old to look after and I had to deal with this.

I can categorically say that while we were married I had no inkling that Roger was seeing someone else. He used to go out without me, and the odd time he wouldn't come home. But he always used to say that he was working late in town, that he was out with a colleague or that he had slept in the flat. He was friendly to everyone but he never flirted with women when he was with me, so I never suspected anything

I had no idea how it was affecting the children. They were so young that their reaction didn't show – they couldn't articulate it. Roger did continue to see them. My mother and my solicitor said I shouldn't let him because of his appalling behaviour, but I couldn't do that to my children. Later they did express their anger and sadness and asked lots of questions, but at the time they took the situation on board with very little reaction. I accommodated him and let him see them regularly and take them on holidays.

After he left, he sent us a letter saying he wasn't going to abandon us. In fairness, he was always there for the children and he saw the children whenever he wanted. It was usually at the weekends. He would always come into the house to pick them up and that annoyed me. When they were quite young I taught them how to telephone him. I said, 'If you ever want to ring Daddy, this is what you should do.' I made sure that there was no horrendous rift between him and them.

Roger rarely supported me or gave me any money.

Occasionally he would give me some maintenance for a few months or the odd lump sum, but then it would stop. He had always run the business and it was all done in cash, so I couldn't access an account for money for myself. He was taking women out all the time but I could never prove he had anything.

When he got more settled with a new girlfriend, he brought the children over to stay with them. He must have ended the relationship with the mother of his child, because he never talked about her. I got so angry that I would pull the house apart when he took them to stay with his new girlfriend and her children, but I never reacted in front of the children.

I have wondered over the years who on earth I was married to. I think Roger saw me as an opportunity because my family were well off and I had a lot more than he did. But I do believe he was in love with me; he wasn't leading me on entirely. It's very hard to know what he really was. I don't think there was a core to him. He must have had no conscience to have done what he did. My friends can analyse him better than I can. They say they saw things in him that I couldn't, and still don't, see. They say he was sly and cunning. I suppose there was nothing behind his charm; there was no substance.

My children enjoyed their time with their father. They got on well with his girlfriend and her children and they all used to go on holidays together. His girlfriend was a good person and we liked each other when we met from time to time. I once said to my children, 'I hope to God he doesn't do to her what he did to me. I wouldn't wish it on my worst enemy.'

My family and the trustee of the estate said that I had to sort things out financially, so I took him to court. My solicitor was pretty bullish and he was adamant that I shouldn't let Roger see the children, but I didn't take his advice. We had an agreement on fees: I would pay 50 per cent before the case and 50 per cent afterwards.

A week before the court date for the judicial separation, I was leaving the solicitor's office late one evening and we were in the lift together. He very assertively asked me to pay all the money for my case up front. It cut me the way he did that. I felt he was putting unfair pressure on me. Maybe he was short of money himself, but it wasn't fair. I wrote to the Law Society afterwards to complain about him because I wasn't happy.

I was very nervous on the day of the case. I was on my own. No one from my family offered to come and I didn't want to involve any of my friends. I felt terribly vulnerable.

My barrister was really good. She was an authoritative woman and I had great belief in her. We drew a judge that she wasn't happy with and we were nervous going before him. Roger hadn't hired a barrister or a solicitor, so he represented himself. It was dreadful. I had to stand in the witness box and be cross-examined by him about my financial situation.

I had a small income from my inheritance, which I had documented in my affidavit of means, and I had my house in the country. The house was in a bit of a state, so my mother had paid for a gardener to help with the upkeep. Roger used that as evidence to show that I was well off, even though I wasn't. The flat in Dublin belonged to my mother so that wasn't part of the proceedings.

The whole process was very fast and businesslike. I let the lawyers do everything because I wouldn't have known where to start. Roger didn't get into the witness box himself for some reason. I don't think he was asked to.

In the end the judge made an order for a judicial separation. I got to keep my house and he had to pay a small amount of maintenance to the children and me. He had to waive all his succession rights over me and I over him.

I never saw any maintenance from Roger and I didn't bother pursuing it. I did try to talk to him about it and be reasonable, but he always said that he had no work. I found out later that he was able to buy a house for himself, so if he did have any money, he was hiding it from me. I looked at the court order later and the maintenance wasn't index-linked, as it should have been. The barrister did ask the judge to make some sort of order in relation to taxes, so that he had to pay the tax on the maintenance before it was paid to me. But it was all irrelevant because he never paid me anything.

I must have been a little off my head after the separation was finalised because one day a friend called over and said she'd heard about a therapy group that might help me. I went along and the woman who ran it was strange and a bit of a hippy, but it was actually good for me. It gave me an opportunity to not feel alone and to be with other people who had problems too. Some of them were married and having lots of difficulties with it. I found everyone in the group to be quite different from me, but it was comforting for a while, until it sort of petered out.

I felt quite isolated in the countryside. Whenever I met new people I had to explain myself because they would say to me, 'Where did you get that accent? You don't sound Irish.' I would say, 'I've lived abroad' or 'My family is originally from England.' I found it difficult to feel at home even though Ireland was exactly that. I think in those days I was very raw and it was easy to upset me. Now I don't care so much.

I decided to move out of the countryside when my children were older, so that it would be easier to get them to school and for me to find work. I was still quite young and had few qualifications so I had to sit tight and look after the children until they were old enough to get themselves to school on their own. When they were ten and twelve I was able to do a FÁS course that prepared me to get back into the workplace.

I could only do the FÁS course because I was paid to do it. I was terribly short of cash. After I'd finished the course I had to cold call all over the place until I got a job. I got my first job as an administrator in an office. I learned a lot when I worked there, not just about work, but about people too. I think because I'd grown up with a privileged background, I didn't think about what I was saying to people sometimes. I probably gave the impression that I was snobbish, because I'd talk about things I took for granted, like linen sheets or going sailing. Other people didn't know where I was coming from.

I worked full-time and had the children to mind as well, so after a year it became impossible. My mother would babysit occasionally and pay for our holidays, but I needed more support than that; I needed someone to come in and help me. I hired a girl to mind the children, but she just put them in front of the television all the time, and they needed more stimulation than that. Those were tough years. They were hard for me and for the children but I can't chastise myself over anything I did. I was fortunate to have the time I had with them, and we get on so well now because of all that time we had together. I do think that if you're going to have children you should be with them. It's something you need to plan for if you're a woman.

After a year of working full-time I went part-time to see how it worked out. The company wanted me to come back and work full-time but I had to say no because of the children. I did some agency work for a few years and then I got a job share.

I went to photography lessons at night. I'd never given up on my photography and I'd continued to take pictures. After years of courses I did a very good portfolio preparation course and sent my portfolio in as part of an application for art college. I was accepted and I couldn't deny myself the opportunity. I decided I'd go to college.

I loved the academic side of the course but I didn't like the way it was run. It was very conceptual and airy-fairy. No one seemed to have any technical ability and I needed to be taught techniques. I wanted to earn money from photography and not discuss it forever. The tutors were all up their backsides and I had a terrible row with one of them. She tried to annihilate me and I didn't take it from her. It upset me a lot and although I did stay on and get my degree I think I should have done better. I now do portrait photography and I love it.

All those years bringing up the children were very lonely. I felt ostracised and found it very hard. One doesn't go out much in 'couple kingdom' when you are separated. I spend most of my time socialising with single people who are widowed, divorced or separated. I have a 'boyfriend' who

I see occasionally, but he's more of a friend than a partner.

I often think that if I was married, people might not be so nosey and inquisitive and confident to say what's on their mind. People ask extraordinary questions or totally ignore the fact that you're separated and act distantly towards you because they know something has happened to you that they can't relate to. It makes you feel a little bit 'other' because they don't get you.

If I was in a marriage I think I would have more confidence. I suppose that could easily be a myth – a lot of married people are downtrodden and at least I am free. There is a huge amount of compromise in marriage and unfortunately it's usually on the woman's side.

It sickens me to be around couples who bicker in company and don't value each other. I think a lot of them don't know that they're doing it. It's a bad habit they've got into and it becomes part of their dynamic. They grind each other down. It's easy to slip into and it's not healthy. I can see it because I'm not in it and I'd rather not be around them.

Roger wants a divorce now but I'm not paying for it. I don't know why he wants one at this stage. He hasn't paid maintenance for years so he can deal with it himself. I'm in a good place now so I don't want to upset myself.

I had some money left after I sold my house in the country and I didn't know what to do with it. I had a boyfriend at the time and he was a financial expert. He put the money in a fund for me that got me an income stream and it set me up nicely for a while. When the economy went downhill he moved the money for me at the right time, so I still have it. It's safe in the post office now. I also got some of my future inheritance from my mother when things got bad a while ago. It's hard to make money from photography and I'm not very employable, so I do need a bit of help now and again.

My children are living in Australia now and I think it's fantastic for them. People say I've done a great job with them. They are confident and balanced, but maybe that's genetic stuff. Of course I'm lonely and I miss them terribly, but they're in contact with me by phone and Skype all the time. We're constantly chatting and I quite like having the house to myself.

There's so much less work now. I'm not using the dishwasher or the washing machine at all. I don't bother cooking as much and I can go out and see my friends more. My 'boyfriend' is nice but eccentric. We see each other from time to time and we have a very nice relationship. We keep each other company on holidays. The children aren't on my mind so much now and I'm not worrying about them. They both have jobs and are looking after themselves and I'm so grateful that they're fine.

I think I tend to shy away from men. I don't meet very many and the ones that I do meet are married. They are inclined to make propositions, especially when they drink. Maybe they think I'm easy prey.

It's difficult because I'm over sixty now. I feel that the next twenty years are going to be what I make of them. It's me on my own. I find that quite frightening sometimes. But I'm never complacent about life because I know that things can change in an instant.

I have a twenty-eight-year-old girlfriend who I met in college and we were having a coffee recently and I told her my age. We get on great and she thinks like me, but I could see she was really shocked by how old I am. Age barriers have come down and the lines aren't drawn as much as they were in the past, so people aren't so aware, but there is a gap. I've experienced so much more than her. I've been on the planet longer than she has and I can't pretend that I'm young because all those years have gone by

You can't reverse ageing but I have friends who get things done to make them look younger. I have thought to myself, 'Am I being a fool by not doing it?' but I know that it doesn't look right. I think that kind of surgery doesn't work because it takes away your personality and the character you've built up through experience.

One is entitled to one's careworn years. Those years are important to your personality and they are what life is about. If you remove them you remove part of yourself and then people are looking at a veneer. Where is the real you? Where is the back up to your story? If you're looking at perfection, then the two parts of you don't gel. If you are just a veneer then you could end up like my ex-husband, with no one knowing what's behind the mask you've put on.

❋ ❋ ❋

One Family

One Family is Ireland's leading national organisation for one-parent families in Ireland. Its aim is to effect positive change and to achieve equality and social inclusion for all one-parent families in Ireland. It provides services and helps one-parent families to have a voice at policy level.

One Family offers a wide range of services to all members of one-parent families including step-parents, grand-parents and non-resident parents. It helps to build strong families by providing childcare, parent mentors, positive parenting courses and family communication courses.

It provides guidance, counselling, a helpline and social support for one-parent families.

One Family: www.onefamily.ie
Helpline: 1890 662212
2 Lower Pembroke Street, Dublin 2.

❋ ❋ ❋

harry

taking the twelve steps

Harry[°] is a shy, reserved man who loves the Irish countryside. He was sent to boarding school when he was eleven. He hated it because he was lonely and was bullied by the other children. He started taking drugs when he was still in school and continued to use while he was in college. Eventually he dropped out of college because of his drug use.

When Harry was in his twenties, he went to study teaching in London. He met Christine and they had a baby. He continued taking drugs until he went to Narcotics Anonymous. He followed the Narcotics Anonymous steps for recovery and managed to beat his addiction. He is now in a new relationship and expecting his second child.

I grew up in the Irish countryside and I enjoyed working on the farm from a very young age. My earliest memories are of feeding the animals – I remember my father would have a big bucket of feed and I would be carrying a small one.

My father grew up in Australia. His parents were sheep farmers. He was educated at a boarding school in England and then he went to university in London. My mother was Irish and met my father while she was working in London.

° Names, occupations, locations and other identifying details have been altered to protect identities

They fell in love and moved to Ireland together. They got married very young and went to work on a farm in the midlands which they eventually bought from the owner.

I was sent to boarding school when I was eleven and I hated it. I was a bit of a loner and I couldn't stand being away from the farm and the dogs. I was lonely and I missed my parents and my freedom.

I didn't get on with most of the kids in boarding school and I was around a whole lot of people I didn't like. The other children were very cruel. I was small and shy and they used to tease me because I had red hair. They called me 'ginger' and 'carrot head'. I was very hurt by the teasing and I couldn't express myself well.

My family weren't demonstrative. It was a loving family but feelings weren't openly expressed. There wasn't great communication between my parents and us children; there was a divide. I was closer to my uncle. He wasn't authoritative and we were able to interact, just as two human beings communicating with each other.

I got into a huge amount of trouble in my last year in school. At the time the whole of sixth year was doing drugs. We were smoking hash, taking acid and speed. I was growing grass at home. Someone in the class got caught and ratted us all out. They couldn't expel the whole year so they expelled a few kids who were the worst offenders. Then they severely punished the rest of us. We were put in detention all the time, weren't allowed off school grounds and we had to do lots of work cleaning the school. The whole year suffered for it but we did okay in the Leaving Cert. Probably better than we would have otherwise because we were kept in and had to study harder.

After I left school there was pressure on me from my parents to go on to further study. I didn't want to study in Dublin because I'd just split up with my girlfriend and I was heartbroken. She was my first real love. She had gone off with my best friend and they had both lied to me about it. I was really hurt and wanted to get away so I wouldn't have to bump into either of them in Dublin.

I went to study arts in Northern Ireland. I hadn't given up taking drugs even after we were caught; I'd just been a lot more careful. When I finished school it was a great relief. I was happy to get away from the shit in school and the loneliness. The restraint of being in school was taken away and I was able to drink and smoke as much as I liked.

I worked at home on the farm for the summer before I went to college. I was getting paid so I went to Dublin every weekend and met up with friends and had wild weekends. I used to take drugs and have lots of fun. Then I'd go back home and work all week again.

I was beginning to act paranoid sometimes when I smoked but I couldn't see it for what it was. I didn't realise that something was wrong with me, and it didn't matter to me if I was crying and afraid to go outside. My life was only about getting high. I had to keep taking the drugs until I got the feelings I wanted to get. I didn't remember the bad times I had on drugs and I didn't care about the damage I was doing to myself. I had to have drugs.

College in Belfast went OK for a while. I was hanging out with a load of local guys and we were all drinking a lot. After a while I began to isolate myself and I was spending more and more time on my own. It got really bad towards the end. I stayed in my room all the time and wouldn't answer the door. I used to buy a bottle of wine in the local off licence and take it back to my room and drink it on my own so I could sleep. My family didn't know what was going on. I didn't talk to them and I would hide it when I went home. I might have looked a bit worse for wear but they couldn't tell.

I dropped out of college in my second year. I rang my uncle one day and told him what was going on and he said to me, 'Just leave everything and come home.' I ran out of Belfast, leaving all my stuff there, and got on a train and came home.

My parents brought me to a psychiatrist and he talked to me for a bit. I don't think he helped me, because I was treated for depression. I was a drug addict and no one realised it. The psychiatrist prescribed Prozac for me, and it was OK in that it numbed me for a while and I stopped drinking and started running and getting fit. I kept working on the farm and I thought things were grand.

I went up to Dublin one weekend and inevitably I relapsed. I did all the same things I had been doing before. Then I got caught in a cycle. I would clean up for a bit and take Prozac for a few months and then I'd relapse again.

I wasn't treating women very well when I went out with them so no real relationships developed. I started a business making apple juice on the farm at one stage when I wasn't taking drugs, but I wasn't paying attention to it and it didn't do well. I would be clean for a while and then I'd meet someone, they would offer me a joint and I'd be off again.

I don't know how my family were taking this. They were very worried about me and they thought I needed to stay off the smoke. I was drinking regularly as well but I don't think they thought this was a problem for me. Drinking was socially acceptable and everyone in my family liked to drink wine. They weren't alcoholics and they could all stop drinking whenever they wanted to.

I was in a cycle that I needed to break so my parents suggested that I do a course and get qualified at something. I applied for a teaching course in London and decided I would travel around America for three months before it started. I was twenty-five at this point.

I headed off to America and worked and travelled around. I was drinking a lot and I was very lonely and insecure. I didn't enjoy myself at all and I was making just enough money to survive. Everywhere I went I would meet people who smoked and I'd buy hash from them and get high.

While I was travelling I met a girl I liked called Christine and we hung out together for a few weeks. She was English and she lived in London. I took her number, thinking I might see her when I went to study teaching.

I think I was pretty screwed up when I came back from America but I didn't do anything about it. I went off to London as planned and started my course. I got in touch with Christine when I got over there and we started a relationship. We were very attracted to each other, perhaps because she was quite damaged herself. Her family had problems and I think she had experienced a lot of instability in her life. At the start of our relationship I was drinking and smoking a lot. My dealer lived across the road and I used to buy an ounce of hash from him every week.

Christine and I were like lost souls clinging to each other for love and security – the things we didn't have. We were two damaged people who were co-dependent on each other. After a few months we moved into a flat together even though the relationship wasn't going great. I was studying and she was working. I was up and down and just about passing my exams.

Our relationship became very stormy. We had lots of fights. Christine would go off and I would pursue her until she came back. She drank a bit but not as much as me. She would have preferred if I wasn't smoking hash but she didn't ask me to stop.

We were very careless about contraception. We didn't use anything and Christine got pregnant two years after we met. I wasn't very in touch with my feelings at the time so I don't remember her telling me she was pregnant. I was trying to avoid feelings at all costs and that was where drink and drugs came in – they helped to numb me.

I obviously wasn't ready to be a father. I had a drug problem and I was in the middle of a teacher-training course. I was fearful about our relationship and frightened by the thought of becoming a father. My parents were on my mind because I felt they would be disappointed that I was having a child out of wedlock.

We didn't think about having a termination because that didn't sit right with either of us. We decided we would go ahead with the pregnancy and tell our parents. I decided I was going to try to sort myself out.

My parents probably just thought, 'Oh God, another problem we're going to have to deal with.' I had kept a lot of what was happening to me from them, and I put on a false face every time I went home. They didn't know the true extent of my problems. I met Christine's parents a few times and I looked down on them because they weren't very well educated and her background was quite rough.

Christine was fine during the pregnancy. She didn't have any problems and she enjoyed it. We were both trying to patch up the cracks in our relationship because we wanted it to work, but there was this spectre of drugs in the background. I became very devious in the way I smoked. I hid it from Christine while she was pregnant. I would sneak a joint when I went to the shops or I would wait until she was out or asleep. I was constantly hiding things from her.

Three months before Mia was due, Christine asked me to go to a Narcotics Anonymous meeting. I went along to the meeting and while I was there I realised that I was an addict. The way the people at the meeting were talking made complete sense to me. They described what I had been doing for ten years of my life. I thought it was great. I finally realised what my problem was. I identified completely with what the people at the meeting were saying and the way their minds worked. No one had ever said anything to me before that came close to describing what I was feeling inside. The guys at the meeting knew what I thought and I knew I was the same as them.

I can still remember everything that was said at that first meeting. I had always wondered why I couldn't stop taking drugs and why I kept going back on them. None of my friends had the same problem as me. I knew there was something different about me and that these guys understood it. The way they described not being able to stop and their thought processes after stopping and starting again were the same as mine. They weren't bad people even though they were leaving a trail of devastation behind them. They just couldn't stop doing what they were doing.

When I came home from that first meeting I was full of bounce and I talked to Christine about being an addict. I said, 'Thank God I finally know what the problem is and I can get it sorted.'

Unfortunately there were lots of things in our relationship that were doing damage besides my addiction. It was a relationship built on co-dependency, fear, dishonesty and domination. I wasn't honest about my drug use, and although I wasn't unfaithful I would often flirt with other women.

Mia's birth was fine but I still hadn't stopped using. After she was born and she and Christine were both settled in the hospital, I went home and went straight to my dealer, who lived below me, and said I needed an alarm clock so I could get up early the next morning to go and see them in the hospital. I ended up drinking and smoking all night with him, and I didn't get to the hospital until the afternoon of the next day. I know my behaviour really hurt Christine.

Mia was really beautiful and healthy when she was born. I was happy but very fearful because I hadn't got my drug use under control. I was going to meetings but I couldn't get my head around giving up. I drank cans of beer and I couldn't understand why I would have to give up drinking as well as drugs. I didn't see it as a problem. The problem was that every time I had a drink I would go and look for drugs. The drink weakened my resolve to stay off drugs and started a craving in me. I loved Mia but I wasn't performing as a dad. My love for her was huge but my love for drugs was stronger.

I thought to myself, 'Here is a child of mine, who should be the most important thing in my life, and there's a block of resin that's more important.' It tore me apart because I knew that it wasn't right but I couldn't do anything about it. It was the way it was. The goodness of the world and everything in it came to mean nothing because of addiction.

I took things day by day. We were surviving and coping. I got lots of help from my parents and Christine was getting social welfare, so we were OK financially. My study was up and down. I was still just about passing my exams.

Three months after Mia was born, Christine asked me to leave. It was easier for her to do things without me around. I had another love in my life, which was drugs, and I hadn't got a handle on things. The fact that she asked me to leave moved me to do something. Her actions hurt me so much that they actually saved me, so I credit her with saving my life.

I was devastated not to be able to see Mia every day. She was beautiful and I loved her to bits. I was constantly fighting with myself and asking myself, 'What is so wrong with me that I love drugs more than her?' A couple of students in my class took pity on me and let me sleep on their couch because I'd nowhere to live. I fell into a bad depression for about a week where I just lay on the couch and didn't eat.

I kept studying and seeing Mia but it took me another three years to get myself together. I'd stop using and drinking for a few months and then I'd feel better, study and spend lots of time with Mia. I'd get back into my relationship with Christine and we'd be together for a brief time. Then I'd slip back and everything would fall apart again. I was falling back into drink and drugs for different reasons: I'd be feeling sorry for myself that I wasn't living with Mia and Christine; If I did well in an exam I'd go out and celebrate and end up using; I was taking drugs to avoid my negative feelings at all costs and I was trying to enhance my good feelings by drinking. As soon as I had a drink I'd be on the phone, ringing around looking for some dope.

It was very hard for Christine. She'd see me doing well and she'd start feeling positive about things. Then I would crash and she'd find out that I was lying. My dishonesty damaged our relationship. She allowed me to have Mia over for weekends and I would lie to her and say I wasn't using drugs. Then when she left I'd have a joint while Mia was there.

Christine was very good about access. She never made a big deal about it. The only time she ever refused me was when I was using or lying about using when I was with Mia. She would say that if it continued she wouldn't allow me to see Mia or that she would only let me see her if I was supervised.

I gave up drugs when Mia was three. I was going to meetings all the time and eventually it filtered through. I had to change everything in my life. I had to do the steps. I remember my last day using drugs. I was sitting in my flat and I was thinking that I couldn't go on. I was either going to end my life or go mad.

If you keep taking drugs and you don't change and you don't understand why you are doing it, it hurts you. It takes away your character and your principles and leaves you with nothing. Life is an endless cycle of pain. The only thing that stopped me from killing myself was Mia.

I got a sponsor to help me give up. He was cool. He didn't get too involved in the whole self-pity stuff. He just said to me, 'This is what you have to do, so get on and do it.' The first few months were fairly tough. I took the first step in the programme by admitting I was powerless over my addiction and that my life was unmanageable. I began to realise what powerlessness and addiction meant to me. I knew that I was unable to give up drugs by myself, so I needed to find a power that was greater than myself. The 'higher power' is a loving, caring, non-judgmental power. It's not necessarily a religious thing. Once I realised that there was something else in my life, I gave myself over to it and I've lived by Narcotics Anonymous principles ever since.

My relationships with everyone changed after I got clean. It took a while, though. I had problems with Christine because of trust issues – I had done a lot of damage by using and lying in a relationship that was fragile to begin with.

The most important change I made was to myself. I knew I had a problem and it was not of my own making. But I did have a choice about what I wanted to do. I could choose to continue as an addict and keep going through a cycle of pain and contempt, or I could go forward and create the life that I'd always wanted for myself. It was all new ground but stuff began to click for me. I believe that the grace of God came into my life and made me realise I was a drug addict. It clicks for some people and not for others. It's not easy to truly admit you're an addict. Some people say they are addicts but they are just paying lip service. You have to accept it deep down.

I can't work out why some people can get clean and stay clean but the majority don't. I've been at meetings for nine years and I've noticed that the majority of people don't make it. I think it's about surrendering – giving up and admitting that you don't have all the answers, and letting go. The admission doesn't go deep into your psyche until you're really beaten, then a window opens and it's up to you to change. It works for some but others will slip back. Something fundamental happened to me and everyone who knew me recognised that.

I was hoping when I gave up that I would be able to repair my relationship with Christine. I wanted to live with Mia in a nuclear family. I knew there were lots of problems with our relationship but I thought being clean would help. She had her own family troubles but I still loved her and had a lot of compassion for her.

I put my best foot forward and told Christine that I would change and that we could get back together. We ended up arguing all the time. She kept bringing up stuff I'd done while I was using. I'd been out with other women and I'd had one-night stands while we were on and off again and she couldn't forgive me. Things never gelled for us.

My family knew I was going to meetings. I think they were pleased when they saw I was changing, but they never knew the full extent of my problems. I was in London most of the time so they were protected from it all.

When Mia was four I decided I was going to move back to Ireland. I'd finished my teacher training and I'd been working in London as a teacher for a year. An opportunity arose for a teaching job in the Irish countryside and I decided I wanted to take it. I couldn't live in London any more. I didn't enjoy it; it was too busy, too fast and work was stressful. I wanted to be in Ireland where I could do the things I loved: walk, fish, be in the countryside or get into my car and be by the sea in half an hour.

It was a definite lifestyle choice. I did have a good job in London but I wanted to be in Ireland. It was a very difficult decision to make. I wanted to keep my relationship with Mia strong so I decided I'd do that by coming over to see her in London on a regular basis. When I was living in London I saw Mia every weekend and once during the week. By moving to Ireland I wasn't going to see her so often.

I told Christine I'd come over every fortnight and spend the weekend with Mia. I had a friend in London who would put me up. The decision was about what was best for me and what would make me happy. It was a really tough choice to make and I felt huge guilt. I also still had feelings for Christine and some hope that we'd get back together.

Christine was very upset when I left London. She was afraid that I would lose touch with Mia. She thought I wouldn't turn up or I'd push out the visits. It took a bit of time of me coming over regularly before she was OK with it. I was seeing Mia when I said I would and Christine eventually accepted that I was committed.

We sorted out the maintenance as well. She was on welfare and I paid money through the child support agency. I also gave her lots of extras like clothes and things for Mia.

After five years back in Ireland I met my wife, Jane. I knew she had the hots for me and we started off very slowly. I had to be careful because we live in a small village. Our first date was a jog on the beach and we talked loads and got to know each other. She's totally different from Christine – very grounded, motivated and well educated.

We're expecting a baby and I'm completely relaxed and chilled about it. It's so different now. I'm thirty-nine and working. I have a routine. Having a baby is like, 'Oh my God, here I go again!' I'm happy with my life and I always wanted more kids but I probably would have liked to have them when I was younger. At the moment it's not affecting me but I'm sure my parenting skills will be ignited as soon as the baby comes along.

There's tension between Mia and Jane. They are both used to having me completely to themselves so they're both a little put out and annoyed. They need to get to know each other.

Mia is cool because she's always been encouraged to express her feelings. She knew when Jane and I got married that a baby would probably be on the cards. I asked her how she felt about that and her only concerns were that it might affect her relationship with me or that it might stop me coming over to London to see her. Once I'd talked to her about it I was able to allay her fears.

Christine has been great. She's always encouraged Mia to express herself and she manages to get me involved in helping Mia if she has any problems at school. She trusts me now. I've always done exactly what I say I'm going to do. I went over to England every two weeks for about a year and then it got too much for me. I couldn't keep travelling over so often. I discussed it with Christine and I changed it to every three weeks and that's worked out fine.

I take Mia on holidays and it's great. She knows I love seeing her and we enjoy the time we spend together. We have lots of fun and she always gets a straight answer from me to her questions. When she comes over here she loves her Irish cousins and they all play really well together. They treat her like a little sister.

I've done the other Narcotics Anonymous steps and they all interlock. It's a process and it works for me. After I had given up drugs and accepted I was powerless, I developed a conscious contact with a higher power. I needed that loving force that was bigger than myself. I started to do the right thing and developed my consciousness and moved away from what was my will and towards God's will. I looked at myself and asked myself why I did certain things. I did this with my sponsor so I could understand my motivation. I then tried to get rid of as many of my defects as possible. In time I cleared away the wreckage and guilt. I made amends to people and tried not to build up resentments that might fester.

It's a different way of living and I know it doesn't work for everyone. I had to develop a contact with God and give myself over to my sponsor. I help others now by being a sponsor too. It's tough to find people who are willing to do the steps. People don't want to change and that is what is needed. It's huge but you're not doing it on your own – that's where God comes in.

Before all this happened I wouldn't have had a conscious contact with God. When I gave up using, God helped me and gave me the faith that it was all going to be OK. You have to do your recovery in blind faith. You have to believe that if you put the effort in, it will all work out, and that takes courage. In my case I didn't have any choice. I needed to do it for myself because I was in so much personal pain. I didn't do it for my family or anybody else; I did it because I believed I would die or go mad if I didn't do it.

Families tend to enable addicts. They shouldn't do that. If you're with an addict, you should protect your family unit from his or her destructive force. There is no way you can get them to go for treatment or to a psychologist unless that person wants to do it for themselves. Even when people do recover, they don't necessarily suddenly become nice people. They can still be damaged and they can still do damage.

These are the Narcotics Anonymous principles that made my recovery possible:

1. I admitted that I was powerless over my addiction, that my life had become unmanageable.
2. I came to believe that a power greater than myself could restore me to sanity.
3. I made a decision to turn my will and my life over to the care of God, *as I understood Him.*
4. I made a searching and fearless moral inventory of myself.
5. I admitted to God, to myself, and to another human being the exact nature of my wrongs.
6. I was entirely ready to have God remove all these defects of character.
7. I humbly asked Him to remove my shortcomings.
8. I made a list of all persons I had harmed, and became willing to make amends to them all.
9. I made direct amends to such people wherever possible, except when to do so would injure them or others.
10. I continued to take personal inventory and when I was wrong, promptly admitted it.
11. I sought through prayer and meditation to improve my conscious contact with God, as I understood Him, praying only for knowledge of His will for me and the power to carry that out.

12. Having had a spiritual awakening as a result of these steps, I try to carry this message to addicts, and to practice these principles in all my affairs.

❋ ❋ ❋

Narcotics Anonymous

Narcotics Anonymous: www.na-ireland.org
Information line: (01) 6728000

❋ ❋ ❋

anna

her own power

Anna[°] is a vibrant woman who seems far younger than her forty-three years. She is funny, charming and intelligent and she tells her story with no bitterness. She had a strange, disconnected childhood and suffered rejection. She had quite a few relationships and had two abortions, aged nineteen and twenty-two, which were traumatic for her.

When she met Simon she thought he was the love of her life. His bad reaction to their unplanned pregnancy devastated her and she found parenting alone difficult and eventually had to give up work and go on welfare benefits.

Anna suffered from depression intermittently throughout her daughter Alice's childhood and sought help from counsellors. Alice is a challenging, gifted child and with the help of counselling and childcare consultants Anna has improved her relationship with Alice and her co-parenting arrangements with Simon.

As a child I was very withdrawn, quiet and shy. I was quite unhappy. I couldn't communicate with my parents. My siblings got on really well so I felt I was the odd one out. I grew up feeling alienated and I didn't enjoy school. I found it

---

° Names, occupations, locations and other identifying details have been altered to protect identities

difficult to live in the real world, so I read most of the time and lived in a world of fantasy.

I was bullied at secondary school. I was quiet and studious and some of the other girls picked on me because I was different. I hated drawing attention to myself and rarely spoke. I was bright, so they called me a teacher's pet. During break and lunch I spent all my time in the library, doing my homework and reading novels. We were allowed to wear our own clothes and I didn't like the high heels and make-up all the other girls wore. I loved worn, comfortable clothes and I dressed like a hippy, so I didn't fit in. I did make a few friends in fifth and sixth year but for most of the time I was on my own.

I was so miserable in school that when I got home I was full of anger and I would throw tantrums to express my pent-up rage. My parents didn't understand me at all. My younger sister was very easy to get on with and pretty. I felt she was the good one in the family and I was the bad one. I wore glasses and had short hair and I didn't think I was attractive. My father said to me one time, 'Being beautiful is so important. You have to be good looking to get on in the world.' I was shocked by that. It made the world feel like a very scary superficial place. When I look back at pictures of myself now, I realise I was very pretty, but I didn't feel it then; I thought I was plain.

My parents were very worried about me when I was sixteen because I was such an introvert. They persuaded my sister to drag me along to a disco and that was great. I started to come out of my shell and had my first exposure to boys and dancing. I thought boys were the most amazing thing in the world and I kept falling in love.

If I liked a boy I was totally tongue-tied around him. I always fancied boys that didn't fancy me or who ended up fancying my friends or my sister. I plucked up the courage to take a boy I really liked to my debs but he wasn't romantically interested in me so I was very disappointed.

I did well in my Leaving Cert and went to college to study English. It was my favourite subject so I was really happy. I had a boyfriend, Stephen, at that time and we were madly in love. He was an amazing guy and we stayed together for five years. We used to do weird things like spend the night in graveyards or sleep on the beach. I thought he was a wonderful being and he thought I was like a fairy from another world.

It was a tempestuous on-and-off relationship, though. Stephen was in a different college from me so we had separate social lives and we were both insecure about that. I would fly into a rage and feel upset and miserable for days about the way he sometimes treated me as if I wasn't there. Sometimes I'd throw things at him. He knew how to trigger my anger and I think he was as screwed up as I was. I think he was terrified of being in love, so he would sometimes try to make me feel like I was nothing. It was such a strange relationship. I think being with him set me up to see relationships in a warped way. My family worried about me when we were together.

When I was nineteen and in my second year in college I had a brief fling with a student in my class. We didn't do anything except kiss. I loved Stephen and wanted to be honest with him so I told him about it. Stephen was furious and devastated about it. He saw it as the height of betrayal and said I had been unfaithful.

Stephen and I had been sleeping together for a few years. I don't think either of us understood fertility and when we slept together we used to use the withdrawal method. Around the time Stephen was angry with me over the kiss I discovered I was pregnant. He refused to own the fact and he insisted that it was not his child. He wouldn't talk to me or help me out. I didn't want to tell my parents and I wanted Stephen to help me get an abortion. He refused to pay for half and in desperation I said if he didn't help me out and come with me I'd tell his parents.

In the end he agreed to pay for half of the expenses and said he would come over to England and pick me up afterwards. He couldn't come with me for the whole trip because he was living at home and he didn't want his parents to find out where he was going. It was all very disorganised.

I had morning sickness during the beginning of my pregnancy and it was quite late – fourteen weeks – by the time I was having the abortion, because I'd ignored my missed periods. I decided to tell my parents I was pregnant and my mother said: 'Well don't expect me to go over with you.' I was very upset at the time; to me it was another rejection, but looking back I think she was concerned and unable to express herself very well, and she was very busy in her life. She had other children and a business to help run with my father. I couldn't expect her to drop everything for me.

I got the boat over to Liverpool by myself and because I looked so young I travelled on a child's ticket. It was one of the most horrible experiences of my life. I wasn't able to do everything in one place. First I had to go to one city and have an initial consultation with a doctor, and then I had to go to another for the abortion. The doctor at the initial consultation was horrible. I felt violated and bullied by the rough way she examined me and she told me I couldn't have an abortion unless I answered her questions in a specific way. I felt traumatised and brutalised by the experience.

I remember sitting on my own in the waiting room after the procedure, waiting for Stephen. I was relieved it was over because I'd got my body back. I had no moral problem with what I'd done, but I was angry and upset that I'd had to go through it on my own and I said to myself: 'I'm going to make him pay for this.' Then Stephen arrived and as soon as I saw him I felt that overwhelming feeling of love for him again. I don't know why I reacted that way. I think it must have been the hormones. We did have a strong connection and we'd been together for a long time, so that was part of it too, I think.

My father picked us up from the ferry and he refused to look at us or speak to us. I felt that this was because he didn't love me and he was ashamed of me. I asked him about it many years later and he said that wasn't it. He said that he couldn't speak because his heart was broken and he thought his precious daughter was irretrievably damaged. He wasn't good at expressing his emotions and couldn't cope with the situation. Physically I had a lot of bleeding and felt awful afterwards but I was too embarrassed to have a check-up when I got back to Dublin.

From this experience I felt that the world was an inhospitable place and that I couldn't trust anyone. I think those events affected the way I later perceived and dealt with relationships.

I worked as an English language teacher in Dublin for

a few years after I graduated. I was good at it and had no problem getting jobs. I liked travelling so I went away and taught English abroad from time to time.

I split up with Stephen when I was twenty-two and later the same year I went to Madrid to meet up with some friends, en route to Paris where I had a job waiting. While I was there I met up with Peter, a guy who'd been in college with me, and we had a brief fling. We spent two weeks together and had a great time. I wasn't on the pill so we used condoms. One night one of the condoms burst and we were both worried about it. I took the morning after pill but it was late in the day by the time I figured out where to get it so I thought there was a possibility I might be pregnant.

I continued on to Paris and soon after I arrived I met Jean-Marc and fell in love with him. I missed my next period. I didn't want Jean-Marc to know what had happened in Madrid, and I felt sure that the pregnancy was because of the burst condom. I tried to get in touch with Peter, but he suspected what I was calling about and refused to take my calls or get in touch. For three days I couldn't contact him. I knew I was in love with Jean-Marc and I wanted to sort out the situation as soon as possible. I did not want to have a baby at twenty-two, with my whole life ahead of me, and with a man I did not love.

Finally Peter answered the phone. He'd been out on a bender, drinking and smoking dope and trying to avoid the situation. He was terrified that I'd want to keep the child, so when I told him what I wanted to do he was relieved. I was really upset that he had been avoiding me and I felt like it was a major rejection. I didn't want him to come to England with me for the abortion and I didn't want to tell my parents either. He gave me some money and I booked into a private clinic in London. I went back to Dublin to see my family and told my parents I was going to stay with a friend for two nights and flew over to London. It was a much less traumatic experience than the first time because the clinic was in one place and the doctors were more sympathetic.

While I was in London a friend, who was going to pick me up from the airport, phoned my house and asked my parents what time my flight was getting in at. That blew my cover. My parents made some phone calls and found out what I was doing in London. They were very upset that I hadn't told them. They were really nice to me on the phone. They asked me why I hadn't told them and said they hoped it went OK and that they were thinking about me. I didn't have a moral problem about having a second abortion, but I was embarrassed about having made the same mistake a second time. It was a privacy issue for me.

I felt as if the world was completely unintelligible. I'd had two abortions and both times the men involved had rejected me, for their own complicated reasons, despite the fact I knew Stephen loved me, and Peter really liked me. And I'd got pregnant just as I met Jean-Marc, a man I really loved. It made me feel that I couldn't trust or rely on men. What a way to start a new relationship!

I went out with Jean-Marc for a few years and I was mad about him, but he was very insecure and didn't treat me very well. We had a brilliant honeymoon period and travelled around Europe, having many adventures, but I found he was all great ideas and words with very little substance, so I lost patience with the relationship. He only fell in love with me after I had fallen out of love with him and had come back to Ireland. It was a period of high drama. A few months later I sent him a letter telling him it was all over and he didn't get it on time. He had followed me back to Ireland, and early one morning arrived at my new flat. I had just started seeing a new man who was waiting upstairs for me. It was too late to salvage our relationship and Jean-Marc left, unable to believe it was over, and trying several times over the subsequent years to get back with me.

After that I went through a series of brief relationships that didn't last. I know I was searching for happiness through another person. I was brought up to believe that the love of another person would make me happy. I was very unhappy and I know I drank too much when I was young. I discovered alcohol when I was sixteen and took to it like a duck to water. I only ever felt normal or confident in social situations when I drank and I can say that all my relationships were fuelled by alcohol. I had all my first sexual encounters with men when I was drunk. I didn't have good sex until I was in my thirties. I didn't know or understand what an orgasm was when I was in my twenties. Now that I'm in my forties, sex has become so much more than just the act itself, and continues to transform itself into something hugely satisfying and deeply erotic.

I was so needy when I was young. I thought that a relationship would save me. When I fell in love I would demand everything from the other person. I wanted to be with them all the time. I wanted to be reassured and told I was loved. I had no sense of myself and no boundaries throughout my teens, twenties and most of my thirties. I only seriously started looking at my issues in my late thirties and now I can see how I am in the world. All my life I've been attracted to men who were wild, messed up and not very kind, not because they were unkind people, but because they had so many issues. And the kind men, the safe, reliable men, I inevitably left after a short time, feeling bored. I was addicted to the adrenaline of passion and drama.

Simon was an artist and I met him when we were in college, where we had a brief fling. When I was thirty we started seeing each other and it was one of the most intense relationships of them all. He was very charismatic. He blew me away and I was completely infatuated with him and thought that he was the one. I loved his originality, wildness and nuttiness. He was totally different and refused to live by normal conventions. We had a period at the beginning of our relationship of complete bliss. I told Simon what had happened to me before when I had got pregnant, and he said that if it happened again he would stand by me.

We weren't together very long when cracks in the relationship appeared. We started to fight, and nine months into the relationship I discovered I was pregnant. I had come off the pill because it didn't agree with me and we had burst a condom. I told Simon what had happened and he went into shock.

We discussed the pregnancy for a few days and every day he'd change his mind. One day he'd say I should have the baby and he'd stick by me and the next day he'd say, 'I don't know if this is a good idea.' It was a time of the most unbelievable, unremitting unhappiness. I remember going to bed beside a man I loved, feeling vulnerable and feeling totally fucked around. One minute he'd say he was going to support me, and the next minute he'd say he didn't want to be involved.

After three weeks of acute distress we met up to talk about it. He looked at me and said: 'I think you should have an abortion.' Inside I curled up and died. It was a final and utter rejection. The difference was that this time I wanted the baby and I felt I was old enough to look after it. I was in my thirties and had just got my first really good job as a junior English lecturer in a prestigious college. This happened at exactly the same time as the pregnancy.

I was devastated and very confused so I made an appointment to see a counsellor. She said that I had to be clear in my own mind that I was going into this pregnancy on my own. My mother, my best friend and Simon had all told me they thought I should have an abortion. I was utterly humiliated and I didn't want to tell my parents Simon had left me so I lied and told them that I had left Simon because he was crazy and that I had decided to parent alone.

My self-esteem and confidence were at an all-time low and Simon's attitude made it worse. He told me he was leaving the country to go to London to paint in a studio and that he would come back before the baby was born. I was very angry and alone, although I did have some close friends who supported me.

At the time I was working full-time in my new job. My employers thought I was fantastic but I was dealing with very bad morning sickness and the trauma of being left again with an unplanned pregnancy. I was afraid to tell them in case they fired me. I thought it was a bit cheeky to say, 'By the way, I'm pregnant,' when I was only in the job for a few weeks. Luckily I could qualify for maternity leave and I felt secure financially because I knew I could take three months' paid leave after my baby was born.

I decided to take three months' unpaid leave on top of my maternity leave. I thought that six months was an OK time to go back to work and that to leave a three-month-old baby in full-time childcare would be a bit bleak. But I knew I would go crazy if I had to stay at home and look after a baby on my own for much longer than that.

I had a very negative upbringing and my own mother used to tell us that we had ruined her chances of going to university and having a successful career. She was an intelligent woman who ended up with four children under seven when she was still in her twenties. She made it clear to us that babies were a burden. She wasn't maternal and didn't shower us with hugs and kisses. She had a husband who was rarely there to help her and during my very early childhood we lived in very straitened circumstances. My father could praise a lot and then be really critical. He used to drink quite a bit too, and when I was young I didn't like being around him after he'd had his nightly bottle of wine.

So I was afraid of the whole 'baby' thing. I had bad parenting role models and I'd never heard anything positive about babies. My mother once said to me that she preferred older kids because she could talk to and relate to them. I'm the same. I struggled with Alice when she was small. The constant feeding and nappy changing were so boring.

My counsellor said I needed to make a plan that didn't include Simon. Part of me was hoping that he would come back in a few months and realise that he did want to be involved. When he was due to come back to Ireland before the end of my pregnancy he rang me and told me that he wasn't coming back. I was devastated all over again. He said he would be there for the birth and that I was to ring him when I went into labour.

I spent a lot of time looking for a crèche while I was pregnant. I was very ignorant and didn't know any of my rights. Nobody told me I was entitled to stuff. I knew I was entitled to maternity leave and lone parent's allowance but I didn't know anything about subsidised crèches or rent allowance. I thought I had to support myself and I felt I had to work as much as possible to pay for an expensive private crèche. I also wanted to work part-time because I felt I should spend some time with my baby. I had this vision of how things would be when she was born.

I went into labour very late at night while I was relaxing in a friend's house. I'd been so wound up during the pregnancy and I hadn't drunk or smoked at all. That night I decided I would chill out and have a glass of wine and smoke a cigarette. Then my waters broke. I was three weeks early. My friend brought me to the hospital. I rang my mother, my sister and Simon in his studio in London from the public pay phone in the hospital. Simon said: 'Are you sure you're in labour?' I could feel the contractions coming and I assured him I was. He said he'd be in Ireland as soon as he could. My sister said she would come but she needed a few hours to organise her children and get to the hospital as she lived in the countryside. My mother didn't offer to come in until the next morning.

I felt completely unsupported and alone for the first few hours of my labour. I was terrified. It was uncharted territory and I wished my mother had offered to come in, but she hadn't and I wasn't going to ask her. I didn't want someone there who didn't want to be there.

The next morning I was in a lot of pain. There was no bed for me and I had to sit on a chair in the public corridor and I was in a terrible state. My mother eventually came in but she wasn't much help. When Simon arrived he realised that I was upset and in a lot of pain, so he started ordering people around and he got me into a private room. My sister came and she was brilliant. She was beside me for the birth and the others went downstairs to the waiting room. Simon came in at one stage but I told him to get the fuck out. I didn't want a person who had fucked my head around so much to be in the room while I was giving birth.

Labour was agony but I refused to take any painkilling drugs. I was a single parent and I knew that taking drugs might make my recovery longer or make bonding more difficult. The stakes were high and I didn't want to do anything that might affect the baby or me. I was screaming my head off and the ward sister came in and said, 'This is ridiculous. Give her an injection.' My sister knew I didn't want any drugs and, as I was beyond speech, she fought my corner for me. I had no interventions and no complications and Alice was born naturally. I was shocked when I saw her – she was big, purple and a bit oxygen deprived. I then experienced a huge high. I held her and felt so brilliant. After that my body went into shock, and I shook uncontrollably for a short time. There's a great photograph of Simon holding Alice after she was born. He looks totally bemused.

I wanted to stay in hospital as long as possible because I didn't want to go home and be on my own with a new baby. The hospital was boiling hot and the food was terrible but there was lots of support for me. I was able to hand Alice over to the nurses and my meals were prepared for me. Simon did call to the hospital regularly but I don't remember communicating with him very much. I stayed for about a week until they said I had to go.

When I got back to my flat, my parents and my sister had organised everything for me. Alice had everyone's hand-me-down stuff in her room. Simon said he would come and stay in my flat for a few weeks and help out, and, stupidly, I agreed. I was still in love with him and I was hoping we would get back together.

The first evening we were back in the flat with Alice, Simon said to me, 'I'm just going to go out for a few hours.' He went out and left me on my own. I was upset that he'd left me on the first night and I started to shake and get very frightened of being on my own with Alice. I was shaking so much that I couldn't walk. I dragged myself to the phone and rang my mother. I was incoherent with fear. My mother said that it was OK and it was normal and I should go to bed and I'd be fine in the morning. I understand that she didn't mean to upset me. I suppose the last thing she wanted to do was to drive across the city and hold a baby for me. I crawled back to bed and eventually fell asleep.

Simon did a bit of cooking but he refused to help with Alice. He wouldn't change nappies or clean up. He said it was women's work, which was unbelievable because it was the twentieth century and we were the same generation. Simon staying with us was an unmitigated disaster. I was absolutely exhausted and trying to breast-feed and was in agonising pain from cracked nipples. I was appalled at Simon's behaviour. I had this man in my private space, who was messy, dirty and refused to help me. It felt like I was looking after two babies.

After a couple of weeks I told Simon to leave. We were fighting, the situation was awful and he wasn't helping matters. I couldn't believe how badly he was behaving so I blocked out my feelings for him and asked him to go. He stayed in Dublin for a few weeks after that and then he said he had to go back to England. He said he would pay me £40 per week as maintenance for Alice. I remember that it just about covered the cost of nappies. I knew he had hardly any money and he was being as generous as he could, so I didn't say anything.

I remember one occasion when I felt pure happiness when Alice was young. I was walking along the canal with my mother when she was three weeks old and I think I was still on a high after giving birth. I said, 'Mum, you never told me that having a baby could be so wonderful.' I'm sure there were many other nice moments but sadly it's the difficult times I remember most clearly.

I went back to work when Alice was six months old. Things got worse and worse. I was suffering from post-natal depression and I was exhausted. When I went back to work I was so relieved to be away from her. I couldn't ask friends for more support because it's hard to ask people to take your baby. I got more and more tired and depressed. I remember feeling like I was in a cage and I couldn't escape.

I went for post-natal counselling when Alice was seven months old. My friends told me I should go and I found it very helpful. I was working and this helped me keep my sanity. I asked my employers for longer hours because I needed more money for childcare so I was working four days a week at that point.

When Alice was one I think I had a nervous breakdown

from stress, lack of support and lack of sleep. She used to scream and scream every night. I had bungled the sleep training completely. She wanted my attention because she hadn't seen me all day and she was very stubborn, so when she cried she wouldn't stop. I was very determined as well so I wouldn't go to her. She would scream for a lot of the night and I would usually wake up five times a night.

I eventually managed to train Alice to sleep when she was two by doing controlled crying and reassuring for a period of time with the help of my sister. It did help and I started to get more sleep but there were always nights when she refused to go to sleep and there was a power struggle between us. She wanted my attention and I couldn't give it because I was too exhausted. The whole thing was awful. Simon only saw her intermittently for those first two years. To him she was just a baby and not a person yet.

A public health nurse came to see me and she helped me to get organised. She told me about rent allowance and subsidised crèches so I left my job and took benefits instead. I volunteered part-time, working at an organic food co-operative. The women who worked there were incredibly supportive and they saved my life. For the first time ever I felt I was getting the support I'd been lacking for so long.

My parents were shocked that I'd given up my good lecturing job and was working voluntarily for this 'hippy' organisation. My mother was very upset that I was living on benefits. She didn't see mothering as a worthwhile job. She saw it as drudgery and so did I. That was why I had been so eager to get back to my job. I also needed to work for social status because I felt other people didn't value you if you were 'just' a mother.

I felt like I had started a new life when I got the rent allowance, subsidised crèche and co-operative job. Things got so much better. We had this ritual in work where we would all sit down together at lunchtime and talk about how we were feeling and offer each other support and help.

The crèche was fantastic. It cost £12 per week as opposed to the £100 per week I had been paying. The people who worked there were hugely supportive and there were lots of single mothers using the crèche who I liked and got on very well with. The crèche organised activities and social events, art and cooking workshops and I made some really good friends. We exchanged our stories and I realised that all these other women had it much harder than me. They had drunks and drug addicts in their lives, beating them up and beating their children. There were really nice women there who were being treated like shit. It was quite an eye opener.

The staff at the crèche saw that I was struggling with Alice so they organised a psychology student from a private counselling organisation to come to my house to help me with parenting. I was a guinea pig for her training with them. It was great because normally that kind of therapy costs a lot and I got it for free. The student was in her final year of training and I found it extremely helpful. She came to the house several times and videoed me and then played it back to me and gave me lots of advice. I went back to her for help a couple of years later and she helped me again and didn't charge me. It was very kind of her.

When it was time for Alice to start school, I wasn't getting on with Simon – there was a lot of resentment and anger on my part. I felt he should be more involved with Alice. He was seeing her for a couple of days every two months at this point, and I thought he should be paying more towards her maintenance.

I had to move Alice out of her new junior school because she was not getting on with her teacher. Every day the teacher came to me and said that she wasn't behaving and that she had to do as she was told. Also, the school day was too short to suit my hours at the co-op; it started at nine and ended at one o'clock and I couldn't afford to pay a childminder the extra hour and a half I needed.

I moved Alice to another school that had a longer day, finishing at 3 p.m., and the principal of the school, an intelligent, kind woman, seemed to understand that I needed support. Simon, who was back in Dublin briefly, came along to a meeting with the principal as he was beginning to show an interest in Alice's education. I remember we were both sitting with the principal and Simon was behaving as if he was mainly in charge of Alice. He was doing all the talking and I was sitting there thinking, 'Why is he spouting off as if he's the one doing all the parenting?'

He did the same thing when Alice had to have an operation in hospital. She was only allowed to have one parent with her in the operating theatre and he insisted on going. I was too tired to argue the point, but it annoyed me that he thought he could barge in on important occasions and take charge.

From the time Alice was two until she was six, I had two relationships that both ended in disaster. I still believed 'another' could make me happy. I got very depressed when each relationship ended. When Alice was six I had a minor breakdown after a relationship ended. The guy was really nice and we never argued or anything. I couldn't understand what had gone wrong. After three months together he told me he needed some space. Today he is a good friend, and recently I asked him to tell me the real reason he left me and he said it was because I was so negative. I was looking after Alice full-time and I was very needy and clingy.

I was struggling with Alice and she used to get very angry and become uncontrollable. One time it got too physical and I pushed her away. She fell and grazed her face. I was shocked by what I had done and I rang a lone parents' organisation and said I needed help. They arranged for me to see someone within two weeks and the counsellor I saw was very kind and supportive. She told me that I needed a break from Alice for a short period.

Simon came back from London and took Alice away for two weeks and he decided at that point that he was going to stay in Dublin. He said he would help more, but he wanted to axe the maintenance he was paying me. I got really angry. I'd been looking after Alice for six years and now he was going to take her one day a week and he wanted to cut the small amount of money he was giving me, which was still only £40 a week. He behaved like an asshole and I know he regrets it today. I told him I'd prefer to keep the money and he could continue seeing Alice once a month.

Around this time Simon met a woman who had a seven-year-old child and they got very involved with each other. He told me that they were going to move in together. To me this was the ultimate insult. I thought: 'How dare you take on another child when you can't even parent your own?' He realised he couldn't justify his position so he suggested that he would take Alice half the time and I would have her the other half of the time and the maintenance would be stopped. I jumped at the opportunity. It freed me up a lot. So when Alice was six, Simon really came into her life. He lived with his girlfriend for a while but they fought a lot of the time and the kids didn't get on. After a year they broke up.

Around this time I became involved with Ben. We were together for four years and it was another very tempestuous relationship. He was a quiet, introverted guy who didn't like to talk much and was very calm and self-sufficient. That didn't work for me. I needed to be able to discuss my feelings. He needed calm and quiet, not a drama queen. I was passionate and full of emotional outbursts and exaggeration but I was, once again, devastated when he left me.

My relationship with Alice was not good around the time she was seven and eight. Things were getting worse and there was a constant power struggle between us. She was having age-inappropriate tantrums and getting into a lot of trouble in school. Her teachers were great: they understood that she was very intelligent but frustrated.

She moved to a new school when she was nine because we had moved house. It was incredibly hard. She didn't make any new friends and she was getting into lots of trouble with the teachers. Simon finally realised that Alice had a serious problem. We went to a childcare consultant and she suggested that Alice needed consistency between us all – me, Simon and Ben. We managed to get a routine going that worked. I had been trying to tell Simon that Alice needed to sleep at regular times, wear clean clothes and eat proper, healthy food, but he didn't believe in all that. He allowed her to watch inappropriate DVDs and stay up late at weekends and eat what she liked. The inconsistency caused her a lot of problems.

Simon listened to the childcare consultant and we saw her regularly for two years. He came on board with what I thought about sleep, activities and nutrition and things got better. For my part, I had a problem communicating with Alice; I thought she was trying to piss me off a lot of the time. We would argue about everything. I now realise that she's a very bright and talented kid who lives in a different world to everyone else. She is extremely mathematical and artistic and I'm verbal. It's hard to communicate when you operate in such different ways. When I didn't understand her point of view she would get angry and we'd end up arguing.

When Alice was eleven the school suggested that she see an educational psychologist. We got her assessed and the report said that she is a very bright and gifted child with extraordinary abilities in some areas. She has special needs in other areas and needs stimulation and help with her social skills. The report pointed out her strengths and weaknesses and where she has problems or potential problems. It also suggested that she see a psychologist on a regular basis.

Now Alice is in a special extra-maths programme that's challenging her and she has also joined a computer club. She gets on really well with kids that are on her level, so maybe she has a problem relating to kids that don't share her interests. I've been putting a lot into my relationship with Alice in the past year. Simon and I are sharing the parenting and he is seeing her during the week as well, so it's about 50/50 most of the time.

I fell out of love with Simon when I realised what he was really like; I had fallen in love with my own idealised view of him. Today I think he is a great person and I do enjoy his company; he's also spent many years working through his own issues and has emerged a very different person. There was a while when we didn't communicate very well because he criticised my parenting too much. At the moment it's a good, respectful co-parenting arrangement but it's taken a long, long time to get there.

I feel I'm at a new stage in my life. I've spent the last four years single and haven't had any relationships with men. I've done a huge amount of work on myself with a lot of support and help. I think when something is broken so completely, like I was, it gets to the stage where you really have to look at what is going on. I couldn't keep blaming what was happening to me on my situation as a single parent or the person in my life. I started really looking at myself and at my way of seeing the world. This was helped by a new understanding between my daughter and me. I looked at myself as a mother and as a person – you can't separate the two.

My health had been deteriorating because of the stress in my life so I took that on board and I've really worked on it. I've used everything – meditation, yoga, dance, homeopathy, acupuncture, nutrition, my wonderful counsellor and the support of my friends.

So here I am four years later. I have such a different view of life. I'm much more positive. I've been to the abyss and come out the other side. I can see the bigger picture of life now, whereas before I was always sucked into the detail. I know where I'm going now and my relationships with Alice and Simon are improving all the time.

❋ ❋ ❋

Marte Meo

The Marte Meo (latin for 'with own power') method was developed in the late 1970s by a Dutch educational counsellor, Maria Aarts. She realised that professional therapists had difficulties in explaining children's problems to their parents. She wanted to help parents understand professional information in a practical way, so she developed a method where normal situations with a child are videoed and then discussed afterwards. The Marte Meo organisation was founded in 1987 and aims to teach the method worldwide.

The organisation aims to identify, activate and develop skills to enable and enhance constructive interaction and development. Its central focus is to encourage people to use their own strength to advance and stimulate developmental processes on the part of children, parents and professional caregivers.

The Marte Meo method was introduced to Ireland in 1991. It is a training and intervention programme of communication used by the HSE and voluntary agencies. It uses video footage to provide concrete and detailed information to parents, social workers and other professionals who deal with children who are experiencing challenges, to study child development, developmental processes and how development is supported in daily interaction.

The Health Service Executive: www.hse.ie.
Information Line: 1850 241850
Monday to Saturday 8 a.m. to 8 p.m.
It has offices nationwide.

❋ ❋ ❋

tom

winner takes all

Tom[*] comes across as an energetic, attractive and confident fifty-five-year-old consultant surgeon. He looks as if life has been good to him and it's difficult to imagine him being controlled or bullied by anyone.

He describes his twenty-five-year marriage to Caroline as turbulent and abusive and he is still wondering why it turned out the way it did. He had a difficult, traumatic divorce and is highly critical of his lawyers and of the legal system because he feels he was overcharged and badly advised.

Looking back over everything that happened to him, he feels that he was in an abusive relationship and regrets his marriage. He found it hard to get involved with women after the break-up but he's now happily in a new relationship with a very different type of woman who is relaxed and undemanding.

I grew up in a large family. We lived in an old Georgian mansion on seventy acres in County Limerick. It had a long tree-lined avenue, lots of mature oak trees and stud railings to keep the horses and the cattle in. My father was a surgeon but his real passion was farming, so we kept cattle

---

[*] Names, occupations, locations and other identifying details have been altered to protect identities

and grew sugar beet. All the children helped out around the farm bringing in the hay and looking after the horses. We used to pick blackberries and sloes from the hedges in late summertime and use them to make jam. It sounds idyllic but in fact it was far from it.

My parents were very Victorian in their outlook and seemed to me to have a loveless marriage. I never saw them kiss or hug each other. They were quite strict with my siblings and me and I don't remember them displaying any affection towards us. Treats were few and far between, and if you got bad results in school there was serious trouble at home.

My father worked very hard and he was rarely at home. He was always at the hospital or at work-related meetings. If he wasn't working he was playing golf, horse-riding or socialising. I didn't see very much of him when I was growing up, but I suppose that was relatively normal for the time and I didn't think we were any different from other families.

My mother was tough. She was a strict disciplinarian and would take out the wooden spoon to give us a slap if we misbehaved. There were seven of us children and we were basically left to rear ourselves. My mother would be out a lot, playing bridge and going to French classes. She wasn't much of a cook so the older children used to cook and take care of the younger ones.

We had housekeepers and maids and I was particularly fond of one maid who spoilt me and used to read me stories and show affection towards me. She left to go to America when I was seven and I never saw or heard from her again. I remember being very upset at the time but no one talked to me about it. I suppose that was the way things were in those days.

We were all sent off to boarding school at the age of twelve. I was a very timid child and I was small for my age. Because of this I was severely bullied in my first year, and on one occasion I was held down by the older boys and stripped naked, before they pulled my genitals. This severely traumatised me. I actually met the ringleader years later at a rugby dinner and in front of his wife and friends I said to him, 'Hi, Colm. I haven't seen you in years. I remember you from boarding school. You stripped me naked and pulled at my balls when I was in first year and you were in third year.' You should have seen his face.

By second year I had had a growth spurt and was picked for all the sports teams. I played rugby, cricket and athletics for all the best teams. The bullies stopped bothering me then and I became quite popular with my classmates.

I was the middle child and two of my brothers were in boarding school at the same time as me. But the hierarchy that exists in boarding schools meant that I couldn't really spend time with them because we were in different years. They had their friends and I had mine. Also, being away from home at such a young age made me very independent, and even when I came home on holidays I didn't interact much with my brothers and sisters. We just weren't a close family.

I had lots of girlfriends during my first two years at UCD but I never had sex with any of them, it was just kissing and cuddling. In those days we used to go away to work in factories in England during the summer holidays. One time, when I was nineteen, I was invited to Sunday lunch by a twenty-six-year-old local English girl. When I arrived she introduced me to her mother and her two-year-old child. I immediately thought she was looking for a husband because she had this child and I was so shocked that I ate lunch, made my excuses and left as soon as I could. I went off to meet my mates in The Rose and Crown pub and noticed a very attractive girl in the corner of the pub. She was happy to go off with me and we went to the park for a walk. I was amazed at how forward she was compared to Irish girls at the time and I couldn't believe my luck when we ended up making love later that evening on a park bench. It was my first time and I hadn't realised that it would be so easy - I think that experience made me more confident about my sexual attractiveness to women.

I was in my fourth year at university when I was introduced to Caroline by an ex-girlfriend. She was a very natural-looking, attractive, tall, dark-haired woman. I'm tall and I've always been drawn to tall women. We were instantly attracted to each other and we started going out. During our courtship I thought we had a lot in common. We were both from good backgrounds and I believed we had similar ideals and attitudes towards life.

Caroline's father was a very abusive man and used to beat her and her mother regularly. He worked as a civil servant and looking back on it I think he was an intelligent man who was frustrated and unfulfilled in his job. He took this frustration out on his family. He drank quite a lot and on one occasion he became very abusive and started slapping Caroline and his wife in front of me. I was so shocked that it took me a few seconds to react. I didn't hit him, although looking back now I think I should have. I just pulled him away from Caroline and her mother and made sure that we were rarely in his company again.

Caroline was very organised and controlled, which I liked a lot. When we got married she gave up work and dedicated herself to making our house as clean and tidy as possible. Our four children came along very quickly and in the space of a few years I went from being a newly qualified doctor to being a husband and father of four. It was a huge financial responsibility. We started off in a small house that was manageable, but Caroline wasn't happy with it and she insisted we move to a huge house in Killiney that I couldn't really afford. It was the 1980s, I was trying to get my practice off the ground and I felt under enormous financial pressure.

The house turned out to be a money pit. It looked OK when we bought it, but because it was old, there was always something that needed to be done – a new roof, rewiring, new plumbing – the list was endless. Caroline was responsible for hiring workmen and staff and she was always having problems and fighting with them. I was too busy with work to take much of an interest, so I didn't really want to know. Looking back now I think she was probably in a very stressful situation but I didn't have time to be sympathetic. I just signed the cheques and expected dinner on the table every night.

I worked all hours in the hospital back then – sometimes fifteen or twenty hours a day and weekends. I had a consultancy in a public hospital and a private practice as well, and my patients came first. I didn't have much time for the children when they were young and I suppose I didn't notice because I was so wrapped up in my career. I think that because my relationship with my parents wasn't affectionate, I didn't feel comfortable being very affectionate with my own children.

My wife wasn't very physical or loving with the children and was a strict disciplinarian. I took my cue of how to behave with them from her. In retrospect I think I was wrong to hand over the running of the family to her and I regret that I lost the opportunity to have a closer relationship with my children when they were young.

Caroline was a perfectionist. The house was always immaculate, and because it was a period home the upkeep was astronomical. Only the best would do and she spent a huge amount of money on furniture, and carpets and curtains were changed regularly. She loved designer clothes, expensive holidays, art and antiques and I gave her free reign with our income. She wasn't working outside the home but she kept busy, going to art history classes, supervising the staff and continually redecorating the house. No matter how much I earned, I was always in the red. I had to borrow every year to pay my taxes.

I suppose I tried to keep Caroline happy by letting her spend all my money. She certainly wasn't interested in what I had to offer in terms of affection and closeness. She was a bit like my mother in the way that she was more interested in doing things outside the house and pleasing herself rather than developing a close relationship with me and the children. I always felt the lack of affection from my mother as a child and I knew it was missing from my marriage too. I know now that I am someone who desperately needs physical affection and it was ironic that I married someone who was incapable of giving me any.

After about ten years of marriage I began to feel isolated and unwanted. We had stopped making love, because the children were around us all the time. I wanted to send them to boarding school because I thought it would help build their character and give us some space to have a relationship. But Caroline wouldn't hear of it. I think she was afraid that if the children weren't there, I'd expect her to go out and get a job, but I never suggested that.

We never got a chance to go on holidays on our own as she always insisted we take the children. I felt her main focus was our lifestyle and the children. I was just there to provide financially. I started to look elsewhere for sex and had a series of meaningless affairs. Working in several hospitals meant that there were always available women around. I never felt guilty about sleeping around. It was a purely physical act and in many ways it was an empty experience. I always had affairs with women who were married as well because I didn't want them to have expectations.

At that point in my life I was cut off from my emotions and I'm sure I hurt some feelings, but I was always honest and told the women I was sleeping with that I didn't want a relationship. None of the affairs lasted longer than a few months, because we couldn't go out to dinner or go on holidays together as I was afraid of getting caught.

When all the children had started secondary school, Caroline began to complain that she was getting old and felt unfulfilled. She suspected I was having affairs but she had no proof. She used to accuse me of being unfaithful and we had huge rows. She knew that I liked sex and she hadn't slept with me for years, so what did she expect? She became totally obsessed with her appearance and against my advice she had a series of plastic surgery procedures: breast augmentation, a facelift, a tummy tuck – all of which were painful and did nothing to improve her looks.

I can't explain how, but I knew before it happened that she was planning to leave me when our youngest child left school. Sure enough, the summer after our youngest had done the Leaving Cert, she threw me out. When it finally happened, the kids were actually relieved and they all said they thought it was the best thing for us. There had been so much fighting towards the end that they couldn't bear it. Whenever I was in her presence she would denigrate me, call me a liar, a bad father, a mean person and a poor provider.

I went to live in a flat and was very lonely and miserable. I didn't miss Caroline but I missed family life, such as it was. I felt that she'd used me as a money-making machine. I was always very popular with my colleagues and had loads of friends but she never made an effort to be nice to them. My friends were very critical of her and made it obvious they didn't want to be around her. She had a sharp tongue and could be quite rude.

Personally I think she has psychological problems that stem from her upbringing but she's never discussed them with me. We went to counselling a few times and I tried to address our issues. I know that I wasn't the easiest to get along with because I work too hard and I wasn't great at communicating but she refused point blank to open up about anything the counsellor suggested. She always insisted that she had no problems and that any difficulties in our marriage were my fault. I accept that I was difficult and perhaps this was because I was brought up in a very tough family as well, but at least I was prepared to be open during the sessions and try to work on our marriage.

When I first moved into the flat, I survived on take-out food because I wasn't very good at cooking. I had to learn how to cook because the kids started to come over and have dinner with me once a week. I went to a counsellor who helped me a lot but sometimes I had a real urge to go back and try to work things out with Caroline. I think this was because I was in a co-dependent situation with her and I'd become used to being part of our dysfunctional, abusive relationship. I also loved being part of a family unit and found it hard to cope on my own.

I was very aware of the effect our separation was having on the children, even though they were grown up, and either working or in college. I still felt they needed to be protected so I tried really hard not to discuss Caroline with them or to show my anger in front of them. Still, they're not stupid and I knew they could sense how I felt.

At this time I was still paying all the household bills and Caroline's credit card bills, which were substantial. I had no control over her spending and my finances were getting even more out of control. She had hired an architect to renovate the house and I was worried that I wouldn't be able to continue paying the mortgage or that I'd be sued for not paying the architects and builders. She kept saying I was mean with money and she didn't have enough to live on. I think she wanted total control over our finances because she no longer had any control over me.

I decided that I had to do something about all the money Caroline was spending so I went for a few consultations with solicitors who I believed to be good so that I could stop her from using them. Once they had a consultation with me then she wasn't able to hire them. Eventually I decided to use a well-known solicitor who had a good reputation. I talked with him and he seemed to understand how I wanted to deal with the situation, which was as reasonably and quickly as possible. While we were deciding what to do I got a letter from her solicitor who turned out to be a real bastard. He refused to engage with my solicitor and wouldn't answer letters, go to meetings or negotiate. It was unbelievably frustrating. His obstructionist attitude made the whole process incredibly lengthy.

They went to town on me. There were High Court proceedings, discovery orders and forensic accountants were appointed to look into my practice. It was costing a fortune – not just thousands but tens of thousands. I did everything I could to show them what I was earning but to this day Caroline thinks I lied and that I have piles of money hidden in some off-shore account. The process took years. By the time we were in court we were separated long enough to get divorced. My proceedings had started out as a judicial separation so when I realised I could, I decided to convert them into a divorce application so that I could be finished with the whole thing. I didn't want to ever have to go back to my solicitor or deal with Caroline or her solicitor again.

In actual fact Caroline lied about her financial situation at the time of the divorce. She said she had no savings but I knew she had inherited some money and she took out loads of cash on my credit card, which must have been hidden somewhere. Lots of art and antiques that were in the house disappeared as well, but my solicitor never looked into any of this. To be fair to him I didn't instruct him to because I couldn't face fighting with her about it. I'm sure she built up a nice little fund for herself, but God knows what account it's in.

When our solicitors first started writing letters and things were going down the legal route, I suggested to Caroline that we might go to counselling or mediation to try to sort things out. I asked her to choose the counsellor, which she agreed to do. But when I arrived for the appointment she threw a fit because she'd received a nasty letter from my solicitor that day and she said that I obviously didn't want to sort things out amicably, otherwise I would have told my solicitor to hold off.

Letters were going back and forth between my solicitor and her solicitor and things were incredibly fraught. We were both drinking quite a lot at the time and there were some vicious phone calls and accusations. Eventually I got an answering machine and just stopped answering the phone. I used to delete any messages from Caroline because I couldn't bear to listen to her. I always denied having affairs whenever she asked me because I knew if I admitted to it that I'd never hear the end of it. I only slept with other women for sex and it was meaningless, but I don't think she would have understood my rationale.

Caroline's solicitor refused to negotiate or to settle our separation (which had eventually turned into a divorce) at any stage before it got to the door of the court. I kept asking my solicitor to try to settle things but there was never any agreement from her side. On the day we were due to go to court, our barristers ended up negotiating for the whole day. We didn't sign the agreement until 10 p.m. that night. My solicitor kept saying that if we went into court the case could run for five to seven days, which would cost a huge amount as we both had junior and senior counsel. I took my solicitor's advice and agreed to sign over the family home to her and pay her substantial maintenance.

After the case was over I got a letter from my ex-wife's solicitor with a bill for her legal costs. I had agreed to pay her costs as part of the settlement but I had no idea what they were going to be. Her solicitor wanted over €120,000 for himself, the junior and senior counsels and the forensic accountant. My solicitor advised me to go to the Taxing Master to dispute the fees and ask for a reduction.

The Taxing Master reduced the fees by about €10,000. My solicitor said that this was ridiculous and that I should appeal the decision of the Taxing Master. I was worried that I'd be really screwed on fees if I lost but I went ahead and eventually the fees were reduced by about €30,000. This was fine – until I got a huge bill from my solicitor for all the work he had done in taking the case to the Taxing Master. I had gained nothing and simply ended up paying the money over to my solicitor instead of Caroline's.

In retrospect I feel I was badly advised, and I have a huge problem with the adversarial approach of the legal system. I think the lawyers were only in it to maximise their fees. Caroline's solicitor made the whole thing much worse by refusing to ever meet or negotiate. In the end it was a smart thing for him to do because the longer it went on the more money he made. I know from other cases I've been involved in that solicitors love conflict, especially between businesses and in medical negligence cases. They can sit back while people tear into each other and in the end the only winners are the lawyers.

The whole thing ended up costing me about €250,000 in fees. I blame Caroline, the lawyers and myself. I shouldn't have allowed it to come to that. I certainly should have been more aware of what the costs were going to be in the long term and I should never have agreed to pay her legal fees. I should also have been more forceful when it came to her affidavit of her means. I could have looked into it and discovered that she did have money from an inheritance or accounts that I didn't know about.

There is nothing in the terms of settlement for the divorce that states what will happen when I retire and don't have enough money to keep paying her the same level of maintenance. I suppose I'll have to go back to court to sort that out and pay massive fees to the lawyers all over again.

I don't think the legal profession served us well. There was no attempt to negotiate from Caroline's side and they played hardball all the way. I think they all knew that at the end of the day I was going to pay everyone's fees, so it didn't matter to them who got what. I think I agreed to everything because I was so anxious to get the whole thing over with. It was the end of a long day and I don't think I fully realised the implications of the agreement at the time. The process took five long years and despite the cost I was incredibly relieved when it was over.

I never allowed the stress of the separation and divorce to affect my professional life. When I'm working I just switch off what's happening in my personal life and go in and do it. I never allow anything that's happening at home to affect my ability to work as a surgeon. When I had time off or went on holidays I would binge drink like crazy. That was my release. I have a few golfing buddies, so we'd go off to

Spain or Portugal to let off steam. I would occasionally hire a prostitute if I was in the mood but it was never that great.

I was single for a good few years. I found it difficult to trust women after the divorce and I just had short-term relationships, never getting involved with anyone on a meaningful level. My social life was great: I was invited to all the parties as the spare male and women were throwing themselves at me. My friends all made a great effort to fix me up with women who were widowed, divorced or separated. It was very flattering at the time but I just treated it as a bit of fun.

I'm very good friends with a few married couples who like me to come on holidays with them. One summer I was about to go away to Spain with some old friends. We were all going to share a villa. The weekend before the holiday I was at a dinner party and I was introduced to a tall blonde woman who seemed like great fun. We'd both had loads of wine and we got on like a house on fire. She was a lawyer and was very attractive and intelligent. She listened to my tale of woe and made me laugh that night. On impulse I invited her to join us on the holiday the following week.

As soon as we got on the plane I realised I'd made a terrible mistake. She kept talking about her work and her awful ex-boyfriend and seemed very self-obsessed. She didn't look as well as she had looked at the dinner party and I knew I didn't fancy her and that there was no way we were going to have a relationship.

When we got to the villa, our friends had put us in the same room. I immediately went into the bathroom, got into my swimming trunks and went to the beach for the day. Every evening I stayed up late, drank lots of wine and then crashed out.

After three nights of this she managed to get me alone. She got upset and asked me why I had invited her on the trip. I told her that I thought she was great fun and that we could have a bit of craic on the holiday together. She got annoyed with me and went off in a huff for the day. My friend's wife was annoyed with me as well. When she came back later that evening she seemed to have come to terms with the situation. There were a few dirty looks during the holiday but we survived the rest of the week and I never made that mistake again.

After that I went out with a nurse very briefly. We only went on a couple of dates and I thank God that I didn't sleep with her. I decided I wasn't interested, so I stopped calling her and she went a bit mad. She thought I was really into having a relationship and I wasn't. She kept phoning me and stalked me a bit. She would wait for me outside the hospital and I was worried that she'd turn into a bunny boiler.

Eventually I sat down with her and spelled it out. I told her I was involved with someone else and I didn't want to see her again. She didn't take the rejection very well and wrote me some horrible letters. Fortunately she moved to another hospital, and I stopped getting involved with people I worked with after that. They say you should never shit on your own doorstep.

It was difficult returning to dating after so many years of marriage. I felt that when I got married I was in it for life. I never imagined that I'd be 'out there' again. It was quite easy to meet women and lots of silly things happened, but it was very hard to meet somebody special. I think I had some trust issues because of my experience with Caroline and wasn't open to the women I met for the years leading up to and after my divorce. I was terrified of getting enmeshed with another woman and I was all over the place. I don't think I was in a position to work at a relationship, as I was constantly worried about my financial position and the outcome of the divorce.

When I knew where I was at financially I was more comfortable with myself and life was less fraught. Once the divorce was final I felt huge relief. I could think about having a life for myself. It still took a lot of time before I was ready to give commitment and love to somebody new. The desire to love somebody was always in me but I couldn't express it in my marriage. I thought I was expressing it by being a good provider and fulfilling all of Caroline's wishes. I now know that that is not what a good relationship is about. There has to be communication, trust and caring.

I found what I was looking for with my long-term girlfriend, Tanya. We've been together about three years and she is a great communicator, warm and wonderful. She's a gentle soul and not in the least bit pushy. When we first started seeing each other she never phoned me or seemed madly eager to see me. She's a very cool customer. I liked this because it was a change from all the women my friends kept trying to set me up with.

I immediately felt very relaxed in Tanya's company and I was finally able to have fun with someone who wasn't uptight or needy. She has her own business and an ex-husband, but she never talks much about him. When I met her first I used to go on and on about Caroline and my bad experiences with lawyers. Tanya was very patient and would listen and go through everything with me and sympathise. I felt as though she cared enough to listen and that she was intelligent enough to understand what I'd been through.

What I didn't realise was that I was becoming like a broken record and boring the arse off her. One day, about six months into our relationship, she sat down with me and said, 'I really love you Tom but I can't listen to you complain about the past any more. I think it's time you put it behind you. I've listened to your stories lots of times and I don't really want to hear them any more. Please hire a therapist if you still have things to say.'

Of course Tanya was absolutely right. I'd got a bit stuck in a groove of thinking about the past and I had to move on and stop letting it consume me.

I'm very happy with Tanya now but I never want to get married again. She has three children and it's lovely to be part of a family unit, but she has her house and I have mine. We spend lots of time together but we're both happy to have our own space too.

Tanya didn't introduce me to her children until we had been seeing each other for about a year. I think this was a good idea. It gave us time to get to know each other and see where our relationship was going. Her children are all in secondary school, so they're busy with activities and their own social lives, which gives us time for each other.

I have a very different relationship with Tanya's children than I had with my own. I have to stand back a bit because they're not my kids and I can't impose my views too strongly. They treat me like an uncle or a good family friend. I don't take on a paternal role, because their father is very involved and they don't need that from me.

Tanya has her own views on how to bring up her children – she's very liberal, maybe a bit too mindful of the children's wishes, in my view. The atmosphere in her home is totally different from what I was used to. She's much more casual and warm with her children. Things aren't very organised but I've got used to that and I'm much happier to be with someone who isn't regimented and obsessed with her appearance.

Tanya is very open and friendly with my kids. She doesn't push it or try to get too involved in their lives; she just cooks them a nice dinner on occasion. One of my kids, Helen, didn't accept Tanya at all. Tanya didn't react and remained polite to Helen. She is the youngest and was very put out and angry that I was in a new relationship, and I think she felt it would be disloyal to her mother if she was friendly towards Tanya. Helen refused to see me when I was with Tanya, so I just let the issue slide and saw her on her own. Eventually she came round to the situation and now she gets on well with Tanya. I think it helped that we didn't get married or have any more children. That was probably part of what was bothering Helen.

Some of my friends are in second relationships now and they have very young children in their second family. I think it's so foolish to do this and it can be very hard on the children because they have a much older parent than their friends. Their father might be in his fifties and not have the energy to kick a ball round with them. I don't want to be in the situation where I'm an old-age pensioner picking my child up from the school disco. The chances are you won't be around for your child when they're in their twenties and thirties and you won't be able to give them the financial and emotional support they need. You may even be a burden to them.

I never really see my ex-wife now unless I bump into her in town or we meet at a family occasion. I've no desire to be friends with her but we do have to see each other at graduations and weddings and the like. I still feel unsettled and unhappy in her company. I've heard Caroline claims that she regrets that our marriage ended, but I don't believe that. She never made any effort to make me happy when she was with me.

I don't know why I got into such an abusive relationship. I think I was just young and naive. I think she picked me out in college as marriage material because I was from a good family and had good career prospects. I don't think she ever genuinely loved me.

❋ ❋ ❋

Legal Fees

The Law Society of Ireland is the professional body for the 12,000 solicitors practicing in Ireland. It exercises statutory functions under the Solicitors Acts 1954 to 2008 in relation to the admission, enrolment, discipline and regulation of the solicitors' profession.

By law, your solicitor must give you information about your legal charges – the money you pay for your legal services. He must write down how you are going to be charged for your case. He should tell you exactly how much he is going to charge you and if he cannot, he must provide an estimate and explain how your charges will be worked out.

Solicitors work out their charges based on a number of factors such as: how complicated your case is; how much skill and specialised knowledge is needed; the number of hours the solicitor and staff spend on your case and the value of the transaction involved.

At the end of your case you may have to pay the costs of the other side if: you lose your case; you refuse money paid into court by the other side and the court later awards you less money; you are told by the court to pay the other side's costs; it is part of a settlement agreement.

When you get your bill it should include the professional fee for your solicitor, charges for general expenses such as stationery or postage and VAT. If you are unhappy with the charges you can call your solicitor to discuss it with him or you can complain to the Complaints and Client Relation Section of the Law Society. You can also have your bill 'taxed' (reviewed) by the Taxing Master. He is a court official who will look at your bill and assess it and decide what should be paid.

The Law Society of Ireland: www.lawsociety.ie
Tel: 01 6724800.
Blackhall Place, Dublin 7.

⁂ ⁂ ⁂

clara

I can get out

Clara[*] is a very attractive, energetic, confident and organised woman. There is no way you would believe that she could allow herself to be in an abusive relationship. She met Patrick when she was young and he was her first real boyfriend. She lived with him in Ireland and waited for him at home while he worked in Bahrain.

After a few years Patrick decided to stay in Bahrain permanently. They got married and Clara moved over to live with him and they had two children. During their marriage Patrick was controlling, untrustworthy, unsupportive and selfish.

The family eventually moved back to Ireland and Clara discovered Patrick was having an affair. She was shocked by his deception and realised that Patrick had lied to her throughout their marriage. She went to a counsellor and eventually got up the courage to initiate separation proceedings.

I was a very confident, optimistic outgoing kid. I had lots of fun in school and I was always up for a challenge, but I wasn't very academic. I had the ability to do better and I could have studied harder but I didn't have much faith in my ability to get good marks in exams. My brother was super bright and I felt

---

[*] Names, occupations, locations and other identifying details have been altered to protect identities

as if I was in his shadow. I got enough points to go to college but at the time I didn't feel I was being encouraged to go. My parents wondered if I was up to it.

I was a very popular kid growing up. I had loads of friends and I had some best friends – people I was really close to. The only problem I had was a pathological fear of being on my own. When I was fifteen someone attacked me when I was walking home from school, late one evening. He caught me and held me but I was able to push him off. I ran away, but afterwards I got really panicked about it. I couldn't stay on my own in the house, so I made sure there was always someone with me. If my parents went out I had to have a friend to stay over.

It got so bad that I went to a psychiatrist but the visit did absolutely nothing for me. I was simply told to get over it and get on with things. The result was that I organised my life around that fear quite a lot when I was in my teens and twenties. I only wanted friends who lived nearby; I wouldn't go to London for the summer or to the US on a student visa because I couldn't be sure that there wouldn't be nights where I might be left on my own. The fear was paralysing and I didn't travel and broaden my horizons because of it.

I met Patrick at a disco when I was seventeen. At twenty-two he was a good bit older than me and he seemed completely reliable. He would always call me and be there for me when he said he would. He'd come and stay if I was on my own and he spent a lot of time with my family. Our relationship was different from my friends' relationships. Most of them were going out with boys who were in school or college, but Patrick was working and I was only in fifth year in school.

The relationship was very much on his terms from the beginning. Patrick would tell me when he was free to see me and I would leave it up to him to initiate everything. We had dates every week for a long time. There was plenty of kissing and stuff but nothing else. His life was very compartmentalised – I was the girl he saw at the weekend and on other days he had other activities. He played a lot of tennis and I was never invited out with his tennis buddies. He worked as a hotel manager and I never met the people he worked with. If there were work parties or social events, he wouldn't invite me along. He'd say that it would be boring for me so I never went. I didn't even meet his family until I'd been seeing him for a long time.

I don't know why Patrick didn't include me in things. I think he might have been ashamed of his friends and family and where he lived. He was from an average middle-class background and my family were quite well off by comparison. I think we made him feel self-conscious. I only met his family because it got to a stage where I said to him, 'This is ridiculous. I've been seeing you for years. When can I meet your family?'

Despite the lack of encouragement from my parents I went to college and studied arts management. During my final year we saw each other a lot more. Patrick started to come to my house every evening after work and he would expect me to be there for dinner. He was entertaining, had a good sense of humour and my family liked him, so my mother was happy to have him there.

After I finished college I decided to do a postgraduate course. I don't think I enjoyed my undergraduate years as much as I could have, because if I was socialising it was always with Patrick and not with friends from college. I'd never gone to the student bar or any of the social events. We only started to sleep together when I was twenty-one. It had been a long wait to get to that stage.

One night we were going out to a college ball. I decided I'd wear something that wasn't my usual style – it was quite a short, sexy dress. My mother was getting ready with me and we both stood in front of the full-length mirror in her room. She told me I looked amazing and I was very excited with my new look. I was walking down the stairs when Patrick let himself into the house.

He took one look at me and said, 'Oh Jesus, you're not wearing that.' My mother told me years later that she said in her head, 'Tell him you're wearing it.' She had worked hard to give me the confidence to wear something different. I walked back up the stairs and changed into something else.

We started to argue because I was spending more time with my friends from my course, so I decided to give the relationship a break. Patrick wasn't happy with this at all. When we stopped seeing each other I suddenly felt very liberated. It was as if a weight was off my chest. I thought, 'Thank God, I'm free.' I started hanging out with the gang from my postgraduate course all the time. I went out with a guy in my class I had a crush on, but it didn't work out. I had dipped my toe into a different life and I felt that it wasn't working out for me. I missed Patrick. He had been such a huge part of my life since I was very young. He had become part of my family and I was attracted to the certainty of a person I knew so well. I was very comfortable with him.

When I contacted Patrick two months later, he was very dismissive of me and didn't seem eager to get back with me. He wouldn't sit down and talk to me or return any of my phone calls. I thought I had blown it and that made me more determined to work things out. I thought we had just taken a break and that after being with him for so long I should be allowed to take a break.

When he eventually agreed to take me back I was so relieved that I clung on to him. I spent more time studying and he picked me up from college every day. My life contracted to Patrick and his wishes once again.

After we were together for eight years we moved in together. I was the one who suggested it. I thought it was important that we move to another level in the relationship. I was twenty-five and Patrick was thirty and still living at home. He had a huge difficulty with the idea of moving out. He said he felt I was forcing him and that his parents would disapprove because they were conservative and religious.

When we went ahead and moved in together they were furious and they didn't talk to us for a year. Patrick was angry and said he had to sacrifice a lot to be with me. I think he only moved in with me because I was determined to move out of home and he didn't want me to live with my friends. Even though it would have solved his problem with his parents, he never suggested that we get married.

I was very happy living with Patrick. I thought it was great fun and loved inviting friends around for dinner and parties. All 'our' friends, without exception, were my friends. Patrick's life was still very compartmentalised and he never invited his friends to our home. I thought my friends liked Patrick at the time and they were never critical. Subsequently they all gave me different opinions about him. They actually thought he was controlling, dictatorial and untrustworthy.

After a year of living together the lease on the flat was up. Patrick was offered a position managing a hotel in Bahrain. He said it was a great opportunity to make lots of money very quickly and that he would do it for a year and then come back with enough money for a deposit on a house. I wasn't too keen on the idea but he talked me into it.

Patrick was quite nonchalant about leaving me. He said, 'You'll be fine; I'll be home every so often.' There was no question of me going to Bahrain to live with him. I would have had to marry him if I wanted to get a visa – I couldn't go over as a fiancée.

I stayed living in Dublin in our apartment and I always had a flatmate. If she wasn't going to be there I stayed in my sister's house. I missed Patrick terribly, although I had a reasonable social life. Patrick knew that I was fiercely loyal and not a messer so he didn't worry about me being unfaithful. He rang me every night at bedtime so he knew who I was out with and what time I was getting in.

I met a few guys during the first year Patrick was abroad who suggested going out. I said, 'No, I can't. I'm going out with someone. He's in Bahrain.' The guys used to say, 'How can he be your boyfriend if he's living abroad?'

When Patrick came home he could be very moody and obnoxious. I would always make excuses for him when we were in company. I'd say he was tired from travelling or he was working too hard and missed Ireland. There were also problems with his parents when he came back to see me. They always wanted him to stay with them on his visits home. They disapproved of me and of the fact that we were living together. When he went to see them, they would have huge rows and then he'd come back to me in a foul humour.

He'd take it out on me and give me a lot of verbal abuse. I felt I understood the dynamic and I allowed him to vent his bad humour on me.

He telephoned me every day while he was in Bahrain and things drifted on like that for two years. The next time he came back on a visit we went away for a weekend. I challenged him about his plans and faced him down. I said to him, 'What exactly is happening here?' He said that life was really good in Bahrain and he wasn't sure if he wanted to come back. I was gutted. I decided to give him an ultimatum. I said to him, 'I can't continue to put my life on hold. You have to commit to coming home or that's it. I can't take this any more.'

We both cried our eyes out in the car all the way home. He said to me, 'It's not that simple. I can't come back to Ireland and get a job as good as the one I have in Bahrain. I'm on a career path. If I give up now, I'll have to start all over again.' He said I didn't understand the job market and the economic climate, that I wasn't giving him any room and that he wasn't going to be forced to give up his job.

Patrick left me at the apartment and he went back to his parents' house to say goodbye. He came back and said to me, 'My parents think you're holding me back from a great career. They say that I'm far more intelligent than you and that I'm never going to fulfil my potential if I stay in Ireland with you.'

I couldn't take it. I was so annoyed with his parents' attitude that it fanned a flame in me. I was determined to prove him wrong. There was no way that I was going to lose this person I loved so much and give up everything we'd worked for. I thought that maybe it would be good to go out to Bahrain. I was rebelling against his parents' opinion of me and I was driven to prove him wrong.

The next day I called Patrick and said that I'd decided to go out and live in Bahrain. I was going to apply for a job. I said that if I couldn't live with him I'd be able to see him out there. He knew things were at a make or break stage with our relationship and it was then that we decided we should get married.

Nothing happened quickly. We kept our relationship long distance for another year and planned the wedding. Patrick offered to buy me a big engagement ring but I thought it was important to save money, so I chose a small one. We didn't have a huge wedding – he didn't want any fuss at all. He liked everything to be low key. It was just family and a few close friends but it was nice. I had to face my fear about being alone because I knew there would be times that I'd be on my own over in Bahrain. I thought it would be safe, though, as the ex-pats all live in a community that's virtually crime free.

Patrick liked it when I came out to Bahrain. I wasn't working so I cooked for him and ironed his shirts for work. I was the perfect wife. I went to a few classes and met some really nice women. I wasn't qualified to do the jobs that Europeans were doing out there so I kept busy by volunteering.

I had no car and couldn't drive anywhere so I was often lonely and bored. The first day I got there Patrick left at seven in the morning and didn't come back until midnight. I had to get to know people quickly, otherwise I would have gone mad. It was a strange lifestyle. Everyone knew everyone and they all went to the same clubs and parties.

I got pregnant quite soon after I arrived and I was delighted. I was thirty-one and ready to have a child. Patrick was quite odd about the pregnancy and didn't want me to tell anyone in my family. I agreed and kept it a secret.

I went for a scan in the hospital when I was twelve weeks pregnant and the doctor told me he couldn't see a heartbeat. I didn't understand what he was saying. He told me to go home and said to expect a lot of bleeding. I was devastated. I was in a lot of pain so I went home and I bled for ages. I asked Patrick to take the day off work and stay with me the next day. He said he couldn't, that he had to go and that I was over the worst.

A few hours after he left I was in agony and I couldn't move. I was rolling around on the floor and I was very frightened so I called a friend who lived nearby. She came over immediately with her driver and took me to the hospital.

I had a terrible time when I got there. Patrick's mobile phone was off so I couldn't contact him. There was a lot of waiting around and some very brusque treatment from the doctors. I was given no painkillers and I ended up seeing much more of the miscarriage than I should have. It was hugely upsetting. I complained to the hospital afterwards and wrote a letter describing what had happened. The hospital apologised to me and said that they would retrain their staff to deal differently with miscarriages in future.

After everything I had gone through, I wanted to talk to my family about it. I spoke to them, but they couldn't understand how disappointed I was because they hadn't known I was pregnant. My friends in Bahrain knew and were great, but my family in Dublin couldn't empathise properly because they hadn't shared my excitement about being pregnant. Patrick's parents never called me or acknowledged that anything had happened, which was very hurtful.

We had two children after that and then I suffered another miscarriage. Patrick wasn't great that time either. He really didn't get how I was feeling and he wasn't there for me emotionally. It's an incredibly lonely thing to go through when you are away from your family and friends.

When you're in the shit like that, it's as if you're a mule carrying a burden. In a good marriage you should feel that you are two mules together. The succour you get is from looking across at your partner, helping you to carry half of it. If you look across at your partner and he's carrying nothing, then it's like, 'Oh Jesus, how can I manage this?'

Patrick talked the talk but he never walked the walk. If I was upset or emotional he'd say to me, 'You need to go and get that fixed.' There was a loss of faith on my side. I changed my opinion of him after I had my children. If there was anything that required his input to do with the children he'd act as if he was above it. He wasn't going to get up at night to feed them; he wasn't going to change nappies or bring them to the doctor.

He was no good at the births because he said he couldn't stand blood. When our first child was being born they put a mirror down so I could see her coming out. Patrick couldn't help himself and I saw him having a look. I looked at his face and it had turned green.

When I was giving birth the second time there were some complications and I had to be induced. I was put on an oxytocin drip and it was very painful. I had to stay the night in the hospital and the nurse asked him did he want to sleep in the room with me. He said, 'No, I've got to get back to my child.' This was a total lie because we had a childminder at home.

After Patrick left, I rang home because I wanted him to bring me in some things I needed for the new baby. The childminder told me that he wasn't there. I kept calling her and she said he didn't come back all night. I was very upset and when he arrived in the morning I was hysterical. He said, 'Calm down! What is your problem? Do you think I was out nightclubbing or something? I was at the hotel. I was trying to finish off my work so I'd have some free time with you and the new baby.'

I didn't believe him. A few things happened during those years when the children were young that made me very suspicious. There were times when he obviously wasn't where he said he was going to be. There were strange phone calls. One night a woman rang the house and left a message saying, 'Hi, is Patrick there? Call me back when you get the message.' I didn't know who she was and I asked him about it. He said, 'I have absolutely no idea what you're talking about. Are you crazy? Do you not believe me?' His form of defence was always to attack me.

I was worried about what he was up to. He travelled a lot to the other hotels in the group and I was never sure where he was or who he was with. He was an extremely persuasive guy and he was successful because everyone believed everything he said. I think lying was second nature to him.

It didn't matter what evidence I had, Patrick was able to twist it around and make it seem as if I was in the wrong. He was a master at muddying the waters. He would take every argument to a level where it was too difficult to defend myself against his attacks on me, so I would just forget it. If

I accused him of something, he would get aggressive and say, 'I was with Paul. Here's his number; call him if you don't believe me,' or, 'Call my secretary and ask her about the trip. She booked the tickets.' I never did because I was too embarrassed to go to those lengths.

I couldn't get to the bottom of what was going on, so I discussed my fears with my sister and she said, 'Why don't you get a private detective?' I said that if I did that I might as well admit that my marriage was over.

After our second child was born Patrick began drinking more heavily. He had some friends who were young and single and were in Bahrain on contract for a year. All they wanted to do was drink. Patrick would stay out all night with them, playing poker and drinking his head off. He'd come home the next day and say sorry and we'd be back to square one. I was really afraid he'd get caught drink driving and end up in serious trouble.

One day he did get caught and he had to spend the night in a very nasty jail cell. It scared the shit out of him. He was really ashamed and begged me not to tell anyone what had happened. He was an ordinary middle-class Dublin guy and he wasn't able for prison in Bahrain.

I thought after that incident that he'd be more careful, and he was for a while. But of course he started drinking again. He hadn't learned his lesson. He'd have about seven pints in one night and drive home from wherever he was. I talked to him about going to AA and he said, 'Don't be ridiculous, I'm not an alcoholic.' Even though his drinking had put him in a jail cell he still refused to admit he had a problem.

We were trying to have a third child and I was having

trouble conceiving. I was diagnosed with endometriosis, which was painful, and I had to have surgery. Again, Patrick was unsupportive and he gave me no help with looking after the children. He always used work as an excuse to get out of doing anything with the children and he played tennis a lot with his friends when he wasn't working. I was never invited along to any of his socialising.

In the back of my mind I was worried about everything falling apart while we were in Bahrain. I was scared of what might happen if we separated in an Arab country. Sometimes he would threaten me by saying that he'd take me to court and get sole custody of the kids in Bahrain. I didn't have a clue what my position would be but I thought it would be weak. Whenever things got bad and I said anything about leaving him, he'd say that he would stay in Bahrain with the kids and I'd have to go back to Ireland. He kept the children's passports in his office and I was terrified of my legal position. I had all these worries in the back of my mind all the time we were living in Bahrain.

❋ ❋ ❋

Around the time of the Celtic Tiger, we were hearing great things about the Irish economy, so I suggested that we go home. I thought I really needed to be around my family and friends for some support in case the whole deck of cards came tumbling down. I felt quite threatened throughout our time in Bahrain.

Patrick agreed to come back because the children were getting a bit older and we wanted them to be educated in Ireland. I was optimistic about going home. I thought we might make a fresh start. We'd been together for twenty-two years and I still thought we might make it as a couple.

When we got back to Ireland we had enough money to buy a decent house and I was delighted with the local primary school. It was a huge relief to be home. Patrick was supposed to get a job in Ireland. We had savings but I didn't want to dip into them – I thought we should keep them for the children's school fees and investments. I worked at different jobs to make enough money for our monthly outgoings. We had bought our house outright so at least we didn't have mortgage payments.

Patrick still kept in contact with his friends from Bahrain and made a few trips over there after we got back. He told me he was doing contract work for a month here and there for the hotel group. I believed him and hoped he would soon get a job in Ireland.

When he was away doing contract work, he would phone me every day so I never had to call him. One night while he was supposed to be in Bahrain I got a phone call from a London number. I was surprised because it was late at night and I wasn't expecting a call from anyone. I listened to my mobile and heard a voice message from Patrick. He was talking about being in work in Bahrain. I was very confused because I'd just woken up and I couldn't understand why the London number had come up.

I rang the London number and it was a hotel. I was really suspicious and I was wondering what was going on. I asked the receptionist to put me through to Patrick's room. I said I was his wife. He didn't answer and I kept calling all night.

The next morning I called Patrick's mobile. He asked me what was wrong.

I said, 'Where are you?'

He didn't answer.

I said, 'You've been seen in London with a woman.'

It was a long shot.

He said, 'What do you mean?'

I knew he was trying to figure out how much I knew. Then he admitted it. 'I've been having an affair.'

I nearly fell down and got sick on the kitchen floor. I don't know how I kept it together.

I heard him moving out of the room and going downstairs to another part of the hotel. I asked him loads of questions and lots of things that hadn't made sense to me over the years suddenly became clear.

I had looked at Patrick's credit card bill one day and seen a charge for a jewellery shop in London. I showed it to him and asked what it was for. As far as I knew he hadn't bought anything for me and it wasn't near my birthday or Christmas. He looked at the bill and said, 'Oh my God, that's terrible. It must be credit card fraud.' He picked up the phone and pretended to call the credit card company and proceeded to give out hell to them. I didn't realise it at the time but he was pretending to make the call in front of me – there was nobody at the other end of the line.

Whenever he went to the airport or bought tickets from the travel agent, he never allowed me to come along or to see any of his travel documents. He kept everything locked up in his briefcase. I asked him why and he just said that he had to be security conscious. The lengths he'd gone to to hide his behaviour from me were unbelievable. He acted like a spy from a James Bond movie.

We talked on the phone for about an hour. He was begging me for forgiveness and kept asking me not to tell anyone. He admitted that he hadn't been working in Bahrain since we left there and he'd been wasting our savings on trips to London to meet the woman he'd been seeing. It turned out that she was a nurse that he'd met in Bahrain and he'd been seeing her for years.

I asked him if she knew about me and he said yes. She'd moved back to London around the same time he'd made the decision to move back to Ireland and he'd kept seeing her. I asked him if I could speak to her and he said: 'No, she's innocent in all this.' I told him he had to come back home to Ireland immediately. He said, 'Please don't do anything until I get back.'

The next day I went into work and halfway through the day I collapsed in floods of tears. I told my boss what was happening and she was great; she really looked after me. I kept saying, 'I can't cope; how will I cope?'

I went to see a counsellor on my own to talk about what had happened. She was great. She told me that she thought I was OK and she wasn't worried about me. She told me that I had clarity about what was going on and that I was a strong person. I began to have a vision of myself living with my children in a small house, sitting in my living room, drinking a glass of wine. It didn't seem like such a bad option compared to life with Patrick.

When he got home I told him we had to go to marriage counselling together. Even after what had happened I still hoped we might be able to work it out. He said he was really ashamed and that he wanted to fix things and he agreed to go to counselling. His attitude to counselling was ridiculous. He booked five sessions in a row for five weeks and said that we should be able to work it out by the end of that time. He thought we could do a crash course in fixing our marriage.

I could tell the counsellor disliked Patrick intensely. She asked him a lot of tough questions and he had no answers. She asked him how he thought he was going to fix everything so quickly. He had no answer to that. His answer to everything was, 'I don't know; is that what Clara wants?' He started to make excuses and miss appointments. When he missed his second appointment, the counsellor said there was no point in forcing it. She left it up to him to make the next appointment.

I gave up asking him to go to counselling. I decided that I didn't want to be a second choice or a consolation prize for anyone. If he wasn't going to give it 100 per cent I didn't think there was any point. I told him I wanted a complete break – a trial separation. He said there was no way we were having a trial separation. If I wanted that then he would leave me.

I continued to see the counsellor on my own and she suggested that I bring the kids along to a session. Patrick was very much against it. He insisted on coming along to the session and he was very quiet in front of the kids. The counsellor asked my son if he knew why he was there, and he said, 'I think we're here because Mum and Dad need some help.'

The counsellor took me aside after one session and said to me that she couldn't see us both together any more. She said our relationship was too abusive and that I didn't seem able to cope with his bullying behaviour. She said that I wouldn't stand up to him and she could see that it was affecting my children and that every time he criticised me I let him away with it. She said she couldn't sanction the way he treated me. So that was it. I didn't ask him to come to counselling again, but I kept going on my own with the kids.

Patrick told me that he'd been offered a job in Bahrain with another hotel. He insisted that he wanted to buy a place in London because he would be travelling between London and Bahrain for his new job. He said that he wasn't going to go and live with his girlfriend. I said that was fine but I needed a house to live in. He agreed with that but he wanted to sell our family home so he could buy a place in London. He tried to persuade me that I could live in a tiny house in the middle of nowhere. We disagreed on this and he went back to Bahrain to start his new job.

Bit by bit things got better. There were moments when I felt that I could do it alone. But I knew that I had been on my own for a long time anyway, because when push came to shove Patrick was never there. He didn't help me when the kids were ill, and when I had to take one of them to hospital I ended up asking a neighbour to look after the other. Looking for support from someone who doesn't want to be there for you is pointless.

I realised that things were much better when Patrick wasn't there so we left things open ended. I didn't want things worked out finally at that stage. The more the separation went on the more I believed I'd be OK on my own. He wouldn't give me his address in London or Bahrain and I suspected he was living with his girlfriend but it was too difficult to try to find out what was really going on.

Patrick spent lots of money flying back and forth between London and Dublin. When he came back to our house he acted as if he owned it. In the beginning he slept in my room in our bed. It sounds strange but we were so used to sleeping together that I let him. We just lay there side by side until I went to sleep. One day I came home and I caught him going through all my personal stuff. He was checking my diary, my mobile phone and my medicine cabinet. This worried me and I started to keep all my things in a suitcase in the car to protect my privacy.

Patrick created an online account for the house phone and my mobile phone. He gave out to me one day about the length of time I spent on the phone and he knew so many details that I realised he must have access to my bills. He spoke to me as if I was spending his money and not our money. I called the provider and discovered what he'd been doing. He knew my PIN and all my details so he was able to gain access to my account.

Everything Patrick did pushed me bit by bit towards gathering enough confidence to initiate separation proceedings. I was still seeing my counsellor and that helped too. When I first broached the subject of going to a solicitor to get a separation he said, 'I'm not giving you a separation.' I was so used to him controlling everything that I actually thought that I couldn't get a separation without his permission. I didn't believe I could file for a separation without him agreeing.

My sister said to me, 'What are you going to do?' I was so used to life with Patrick that I actually said to her, 'I don't know; I'll have to ask Patrick.' It was crazy. I really had to steel myself to get the ball rolling. I had to make myself believe that I could get out of my awful situation.

I went to see a well-known family law solicitor and she was incredibly aggressive. She said that we'd screw him and take him to the cleaners. I didn't like her attitude, as I wanted to try to resolve things as amicably as possible. I didn't want to go to war.

I then spoke to a barrister who was a friend of my cousin. She recommended a solicitor who was a lot calmer. I went to see that solicitor and I liked his style. He sent off a letter to Patrick. Things inched along very slowly. I stopped allowing him to sleep in my room and instead, when he came over, he shared a room with one of the children. My solicitor didn't seem to be in a hurry and everything took ages. There were letters going back and forth and I thought we would never get a court date.

There were two years when it seemed nothing at all happened. We tried to get information from Patrick about where he was living and how much money he was making. He was very cagey and it took ages to get even basic information. He was incredibly arrogant and acted as if he was above the law and didn't have to cooperate.

Patrick took the children to Bahrain twice during the two years leading up to the court date. I was terrified. I thought he might try to keep them over there. He had threatened me before and said that he would take the kids over to Bahrain and I'd never see them again. My solicitor told me not to worry and that he was just trying to frighten me. He wouldn't even tell me the exact dates he was going to take them on holidays.

The first time Patrick took them away to Bahrain and London for two weeks he didn't answer his phone the whole time he was away. The kids weren't allowed to call me and I wasn't able to speak to them. I was distraught. I knew they were away with him but I didn't know exactly where they were. My solicitor kept me calm but I was ready to get on the phone to Interpol. The kids were traumatised on that holiday. They were crying when they got home because they were so upset that Patrick hadn't allowed them to call me.

I was still seeing the counsellor with the children and when I told her what had happened on the holiday she took me aside and said she was really concerned about Patrick's behaviour. I think she was in an awkward situation. She didn't think I could protect the children from his emotional abuse. She said she was concerned that the children might be psychologically damaged by his behaviour. She felt that she might have to talk to the HSE about us as a family.

I didn't want a social worker to get involved so I asked her what I should do. She asked if she could meet with my family so she could be sure that I had people around me to support the children and me. They all said that I was getting stronger and that they were there to support me. I knew myself that my resolve to get Patrick out of my life was getting stronger.

When we finally got to court Patrick huffed and puffed during the negotiations. He was full of hot air. He didn't want to go into the courtroom before a judge because it was obvious from the documents he'd been providing that he had told lies to us about his financial situation. We ended up negotiating a settlement that I thought was fair to me. I wasn't responsible for the debts he had run up and I had the house signed over to me. There were certain things in it that weren't clearly spelled out in the agreement, such as the date he was supposed to pay the maintenance each month, and I would have preferred if they had been clarified on the day.

My barrister told me that the agreement to pay maintenance would be difficult to enforce if Patrick was living abroad and got behind with his payments. Of course he never paid on time and I'm still chasing him for months of arrears, and he floats in and out of the kids' lives when he feels like it.

Going through the process has given me backbone that I never had. I have a sense of power and I've become much more positive about things. The best thing about the judicial separation is that Patrick can't come to my house any more. Having him there, looking through my things, was a horrible violation.

I'm with someone new now and he provides me with extra support. If Patrick is being an idiot on the phone I just put Peter on to him and ask him to explain it to him. He's always going to be a bully and I'm not going to allow it any more. There was a big fuss last summer because I told him I was taking the children away to Portugal with Peter. He absolutely freaked out and said that I wasn't allowed to and he was going to stop me. I checked with my solicitor and he said there was nothing Patrick could do but I was worried until we were safely on the plane that a policeman or airport security would try to stop us.

My kids are great. They are really well balanced. They love their father but they also know his faults. I don't have to point them out to them.

I've thought about what I've gone through and I hope that if this ever happens to my daughter, if she gets involved with someone like Patrick, that she won't be scared to leave him. I don't want my child to be in a marriage where she is abused and disrespected. I want her to have a role model, so if she ever finds herself in a similar position, she can look back and say to herself, 'I can get out. My mum had the guts to get herself out of it when she was in her forties.'

I never believed I could go it alone and now I can't believe that I ever believed that!

❋ ❋ ❋

AIM Family Services

AIM is a voluntary organisation that offers non-denominational couple and individual counselling, family mediation and legal information service to people experiencing marital, relationship and family problems.

Its members are professionally trained and accredited counsellors and mediators who offer sliding scale and low cost services to couples. AIM has a free drop-in centre that provides legal advice and information on counselling, mediation and family law.

AIM Family Services: www.aimfamilyservices.ie
Tel: 01 6708363
64 Dame Street, Dublin 2.

❋ ❋ ❋

rory

love to give

Rory* is a dynamic, handsome, intelligent man with a soft Dublin accent. He is interesting, passionate and charismatic. He grew up in difficult circumstances with awful family problems and he left home at a very young age, with little education.

Rory had a child with Natalie when he was nineteen. He tried to stay with her and be a father to their child but she suffered from mental illness and their relationship became impossible.

Rory met another woman and they had two sons together. Their relationship was difficult and they eventually separated and divorced.

He is now living happily with his new partner, with whom he has three children.

I'm from a very poor background. I grew up in inner-city Dublin and my father was an alcoholic. He got married and had all his children when he was very young and he drank all the time. My mother was eighteen when I was born and we never had any money. Mum used to borrow money from her mum when things were very bad. When she did have money she used it to feed us and not herself. She was skin and bone.

My father made my mother's life misery. He was

---

*Names, occupations, locations and other identifying details have been altered to protect identities unfaithful all the time. He would come home from long drinking sessions with lipstick on his collar and she would wash and iron his shirt and he'd go off again.

I didn't know my father very well because he was never around. He was a clever, impressive man. He'd give you a great laugh if you talked to him and he survived out in the world because he sang like a nightingale. He was invited everywhere because he was great fun and a great entertainer. The pub landlords would bring him home when he couldn't get back himself. He was welcome everywhere. He never had a problem getting served at holy hour. He would just knock on the window of a pub and they'd let him in.

He was able to get jobs easily because he was smart. He'd get the job, but he'd only be able to hold it down for a while because he'd go off on a bender or he'd smash up a company car. My mother didn't leave him because it was a different age. I grew up in the 1950s and 60s. People didn't get divorced or separated then. If there had been such thing as divorce I would have forced my mother to get one. There were no women's refuges in those days either. I felt sorry for her but I hated her for picking my father in the first place.

I got no education. I went from primary school to a technical college where I learned woodwork and metalwork. I left before the Inter Cert because I was drinking heavily and wanted to get away from home. I was already drinking bottles of spirits when I was fourteen. I think I was trying to get to know my father.

I went to work on building sites when I was fourteen and I started living away from home as much as I could. I stayed in lots of different places and was hungry a lot of the time. I lived with friends, sleeping under beds so their parents wouldn't know. I lived on the streets before I knew cardboard would keep me warm. I slept in doorways and parks. I slept in the city centre some of the time. I'd hide in Stephen's Green until everyone left the pubs. I didn't want the dirty old guys to get me. The streets would be empty by 11.45 p.m.

The police would try to get me to go home and I would say that I couldn't go because my father was violent. I didn't get on with him and he would hit me when he was there.

I was broke throughout my teens. Then I found a place to live. It was a hippy commune near town where a whole load of us lived together. It was like a squat and no one owned it.

When I was seventeen I started to sell stuff on stalls. I used to make quite a bit of money. We would go out at night and take furniture out of skips and bins and gather it together and sell it at the weekends in markets. I was young and goodlooking and the girls liked me and would flirt with me while I was working.

I had lots of relationships with girls when I was young. I was with different women all the time. I liked women; my best friends were women and I had grown up hanging around with girls.

One weekend I went to party in Wicklow. I was eighteen at the time and that was where I met Natalie. She was a student and she'd missed the bus home. I asked her to stay with me and she took it up differently and we ended up getting together. I made her pregnant immediately. At that age I didn't think about birth control. It never even crossed my mind.

I didn't realise it at the time but Natalie had a history of mental illness. Her pregnancy caused a chemical imbalance and it made it worse. It was one of the worst periods of my life. Natalie became psychotic. After she had our daughter, Isabel, they wouldn't let her out of the hospital because they were watching her carefully. They brought her to a psychiatric ward and they asked me to take our baby. I didn't know what to do. I cried my eyes out and asked my mother to help me and she took Isabel for a while. The doctors at the hospital said: 'The only thing that will help Natalie is your love.'

I was nineteen and I had a good job as a machine operator in a factory at the time. It was dangerous, highly skilled work and very well paid. I was making more than company executives. I tried to look after Natalie and our child for a year but it was too difficult. The symptoms of her illness were so strong. She was awake all night, screaming that demons were trying to get her and people were attacking her. If we went anywhere together she would start talking very strangely and out of context or cause a scene. I couldn't cope with it. It got to me so much. One day I picked her up and put her in a bear hug and put her outside my door and said goodbye. She got on well with her family and I knew she could go to live with them.

Natalie was a lovely girl and a great friend but I acted out of self-preservation. Her friends loved her and she was a very intelligent, kind girl. When she was in college she helped everyone, she was amazing but I had to ask her to leave because I was going mad myself. I told her psychiatrist that I would have to check myself into hospital if it went on. Her family helped her mind Isabel for a while until she came to live with me permanently when she was two.

So I had a year on my own as a bachelor again. I didn't see Natalie or my daughter during that year unless I bumped into them by accident. I felt very damaged by what had happened with her. No person should have to go through that. Her family didn't help because they hassled me all the time. They said I should take responsibility for her and marry her, but I would have gone crazy if I'd done that. I had tried to love her and had put in lots of effort with her but her illness got in the way. I wanted more than anything to give love and receive love because that's the way I am, but it couldn't work with her.

After a year on my own I was in a pub playing poker one evening. This stunning girl called Helen came in. She started playing poker as well. I was hard to beat at poker and so was she. We had a great night. I started telling her about my plan to go travelling to China and I invited her back to my house. We were together very quickly. I didn't think about having a relationship with her. She was just another girl as far as I was concerned.

But Helen did want a relationship and she was pregnant within a month. She moved in with me right away. I decided I wanted everything to be correct this time. I was twenty-two and I had a lot of love in me to give. It was great for a while – very lovey-dovey. Then she got moody and we started to fight a lot. Suddenly her attitude changed and I began to see her in a different light. She became very demanding, pushy and aggressive. She always wanted to know where I was going and what I was doing and she nagged me all the time. She tried to get aggressive and physical with me but I'm a big guy and very strong, so although she was hitting me I could block her punches easily.

I had a lot of nice things in my flat and occasionally when Helen was in a temper she would pick up stuff and smash it to pieces. She was tall, fit and strong. Her brother said to me that he was glad she was with me because I was tough and I'd be able to control her.

Helen wanted to control me and I didn't want to be controlled. I had a lot of different work going on. I was buying and selling electronic stuff and I needed to go out and meet people. I wasn't with anyone else and I always came back.

My daughter Isabel started living with us when she was two and her mum used to see her on a weekly basis. Natalie would upset Isabel and make a show of her if they went out together so it was difficult. I used to see the psychiatrist and social worker once a month and I'd talk to them about how she was.

Natalie's visits with Isabel were supposed to be supervised, but her family lied to me and I know they didn't supervise her. When Isabel was twelve I paid a lot of money to go to see a lawyer to see what I could do. The lawyer was a well-known barrister and she said my daughter didn't have to keep seeing her mum if she didn't want to. From then on Isabel saw her mum only occasionally. Sadly, Natalie died a few years later. She went into hospital when she was sick and I think they couldn't keep her there. She was let out and she died over the weekend in her flat.

Helen and I had a baby boy and we called him Daniel. Helen was working in a very good job at the time so she continued working and I worked from home and minded the children. Isabel was living with us so I had two children to mind. I got on really well with the children when they were small. In every photograph we have of me with the children they are always in my arms. I was more like a mum than a dad. When we had our second child, Patrick, Helen gave up working and I went out and got a few casual building jobs. I was making good money so things were fine.

Helen wanted to get married and she went on about it all the time. She would ask and ask and then I'd say yes and then she would ask when and I wouldn't answer. She would cry her eyes out all the time because it wasn't happening. I eventually said yes and we got married in the local church and had a great party afterwards.

The three children, Helen and I were living in a house that I'd bought cheaply with elderly sitting tenants. No one wanted to buy it because it was in bits and set out in horrible bedsits. I moved in after some students moved out and I had a whole floor to myself. I did lots of building work on the house, rewired it, got a telephone, installed proper central heating and I made it into a really nice place. The sitting tenants were really old so I didn't mind them living there.

After we got married things got worse and worse. Helen became really violent and there were times when I'd sleep out in the shed in the garden with rats, rather than stay with her. I started to hate her. I never hated anyone like I did her. She would freeze me out, withhold affection and not talk to me for months. Sometimes we'd make love all night and she'd ignore me the next day. I think she had problems. She tried to be so tough.

I tried to talk to Helen so many times, I tried to get things back on track but it was impossible. I'd say something to her that we had just discussed and she'd say, 'We never had that conversation.' Her parents' relationship was a mess – they were very cold people, so I think she got it from them.

We split up briefly when the kids were five, eight and twelve. I wasn't with anyone else. She kept threatening to go and live with her sister and I used to say, 'Just go, then.' She went for a while and then she came back. I think I only stayed with her for the kids. I loved them and I wanted them to have stability.

My son Daniel used to fight his mother's battles and after the split she came back with the children and Daniel wouldn't speak to me. He used say to me, 'Why don't you leave? This is our house.' I would say to him, 'No it's not; it's my house.' From the time he was eight until he was sixteen he avoided me and wouldn't talk to me.

I think my son thought the trouble in the marriage was coming from me. I had a building company at the time and I was very, very busy. I would come home after a hard day working and I'd be starving. Helen would be sitting down with the children eating and there would be no food for me. I'd say, 'Fuck you,' and storm out. She knew how to provoke and she was provoking me regularly. I would walk out of the house and go and drink because I'd be so frustrated.

Our relationship was very bad but we still lived together. I was travelling a lot and managing building jobs abroad. I was very lonely and I started to see other women when the children were in their teens.

I met one girl when I was in Copenhagen and we ended up having an affair for a year. She was wild and extroverted and really good-natured. It didn't last because I was still in my marriage and I couldn't commit. I still slept with my wife sometimes and I was honest about it. My girlfriend was in love with me and wanted me to get a separation, but I wasn't ready at that stage. Eventually I saw that there was no point in keeping up the relationship. It wasn't working so we split up.

Helen used to threaten to leave on a regular basis when Isabel was a teenager. Isabel could be quite difficult and they were always arguing. I felt I had to defend Isabel because she had such a hard time growing up and her real mum wasn't around. They had a personality clash and Helen used to say that if Isabel didn't leave, then she would. There was a lot of agro. I used to tell Helen to leave if she wanted to.

My relationship with Helen broke my heart, it really did. I was always searching for the love I didn't get as a child. I had so much love to give and I wasn't getting it or giving it at home with my wife.

I met a really great girl called Emily at an art exhibition and we went out together for about two years. The children were a bit older and I knew I would separate but I didn't know exactly when. The kids still needed me and I didn't want to leave them. Emily's friends tried to split us up. They said, 'He's a married man and he'll never leave his wife.' She was a very sensitive girl and she cried a lot during our relationship.

I was living with Emily about 60 per cent of the time and the rest of the time I was going home to my house to protect my rights and see my children. But it got too much for Emily and she left me. Helen had found out about her and rang her mother and father and called her a home wrecker.

When it ended with Emily I was so depressed. I longed for her affection. I really did love her. She was one of the nicest people I've ever met. I was depressed for four years after it ended. I couldn't believe how low I got. I don't believe in suicide – it's against my beliefs, but I felt like killing myself when that relationship ended. I didn't think happiness would exist for me ever again.

I knew if Helen and I ended our marriage that there wouldn't be enough money to buy us each a house. We were still living in the house with sitting tenants. I knew they weren't well but I couldn't sell the house until they died. It wasn't a suitable house for us long-term because there was no garden and it was really more suited to office use. I wanted to apply for planning permission to convert it to offices and sell it on.

I sat down with Helen and we had a real heart to heart. I said I couldn't take her moodiness and freezing me out for weeks at a time. She treated me as if she couldn't stand me a lot of the time. I kept asking her why she was like that but she couldn't explain it. She wasn't happy with me working late but she fought with me when I was around so I never wanted to come home early. She admitted she had a problem but she couldn't tell me why she behaved the way she did. She said she wanted to work on it, but we didn't go for counselling – it just wasn't something you did in those days.

We made an arrangement with each other. I said that when the sitting tenants were gone that I'd get planning permission to turn the house into offices, sell the building and buy a new house. I didn't know how much money I was going to get. I said that when we moved to the new place we could make a new start and put it all behind us. I made her put her hand on her heart and say that she would do that. She said she meant it and I believed her.

We agreed that if there was any hassle she the she would talk to me and explain what was wrong. I felt that if we went back to the way we were – fighting all the time – our relationship would be over.

The tenants left and went into a nursing home. I got planning permission and I ended up selling the building for quite a lot of money – far more than I had expected. We were able to buy a nice house and we all moved in there to start again.

Peace lasted for six weeks. One morning I got up and Helen wouldn't talk to me. I was wondering what was going on. I didn't say anything because I thought she would realise she was wrong and stop it when I got home that evening. When I got home she turned away from me and wouldn't even look at me. This went on for four weeks.

Helen became impossible again. She would argue all the time. She would start arguments for the sake of it and they would go on for hours. She'd argue that black was white. Eventually you'd agree with her for peace. Then she'd ask, 'Why are you agreeing with me? That's not right,' and she'd start arguing that white was black. She was so fucked up.

I went to see a solicitor and he advised that we go to mediation. Helen made every excuse not to go. She was late or she couldn't find the place. My children had been experiencing all this negativity for years at this stage. My son used to try to get involved and I'd say to him, 'I'm not having this argument with you; it's with your mother. Some day you'll realise what the truth is here.' He started to understand what she was like when he was mature enough to see what was going on.

Helen used to threaten me when we were alone together.

She'd say if we split up I wouldn't be able to see my sons. A lot of her family lived in America so I was afraid she'd go over there and I'd never see them again.

I continued to try to get Helen to go to mediation. Eventually we got to a few meetings with a counsellor but she kept lying to her about everything. I said to the counsellor, 'I find it difficult to sit in a room with Helen. I don't believe one word that's coming out of her mouth.' But I felt that the counsellor believed everything Helen was saying. Everything she said about me was negative: I was having affairs, I was never at home and I didn't pay her any attention. The mediation never worked because she wasn't being honest.

I went back to my solicitor. They're a good firm and they employ great barristers. They always get the best in the field but it still took a long time to get to court because Helen never replied to any of their letters. I moved out of the house then because I had met a girl called Juliet. She was a lovely person and I moved in with her. I didn't want her dragged into all this.

When the case was heard I was looking for a divorce because I said we had been apart for four of the previous five years. I was warned by my barrister that the barrister on the other side was very tough. They made it look as if I had still been living with Helen and that our relationship wasn't over and I didn't get a divorce on the day. I got a judicial separation. The house was divided 50/50.

The judge told me that I could come back in two years and get a divorce. My solicitor had to keep writing to Helen because she wouldn't respond. It was years before I finally got a divorce. My son would push her and say, 'Why won't you get divorced?' Helen said she was not sure why. I think she just wanted to torture me.

Helen stayed living in our family home. My girlfriend didn't want to move in there. I got the house valued and let Helen buy me out. It was a great house and I was sorry to have to do that.

We had drawn up a list of possessions that she was supposed to give back to me. I had all my stuff in that house: paintings, furniture, mirrors, antiques – everything. She argued over everything and insisted that it was all her stuff. I lost thousands of euros worth of my things but it wasn't worth going back into court over it.

Eventually the divorce was finalised. Nothing needed to be renegotiated because we'd done it all during the separation. When we were in court Helen would try to talk to me and I would just walk away. I couldn't stand to talk to her. I think she still had feelings for me. She must have thought she could keep me for ever no matter how much she tortured me.

Just before I met Juliet I was asking myself, 'What can I do today?' I didn't want to go out drinking because I was bored with it and thought that I'd just end up going home with someone. I hadn't sailed for years so I decided I'd go sailing. I thought it would be a safe thing to do. I went to a sailing club and saw Juliet in a boat with another guy. I thought he was her husband.

We were left alone together having a drink and I found out she was single. She hit me very hard very quickly. There was something so attractive about her. She is a beautiful girl with an amazing body and she has this incredible heart. There is something about her that none of the others have and it just clicked. I don't know why she's with me. She's a very well-educated, clever girl and we're from two different planets.

Things with Juliet are excellent now. We have three children together. There is a huge age gap between them and my older children, and I remember bouncing Alison on my knee when she was a few months old and thinking, 'Oh fuck, how have I done this? I've got to go through all those growing up years and all the craziness of the teenage years again.' I love having them, though. I love my kids and it's either going to kill me or keep me young. I hope it will keep me young. I firmly believe age is a concept. I have to keep fit so I can play soccer with these guys. It's good that I'm older because I think kids get on better with older people. There's something reassuring about being in the company of a person who is older and wiser.

Juliet gets on excellently with Isabel, Daniel and Patrick. It's not a stepmother role because they're all adults. She is very organised and loves to cook for them. They all come here for birthdays and Christmas and they love my younger kids. I have a great relationship with all my kids now.

I've read *Men Are from Mars and Women Are from Venus* and I agree with it. Men and women are so different. Men want different things from women. We like to go to the pub and do a bit of male bonding and drink a pint. My wife says to me, 'Why don't you stop in the pub on the way home from work and have a pint?' I think she's the greatest thing ever. I go and chill for a while and then I come back home in good form.

I've always advised people who are in a bad relationship to get out of it. Hell can be in your own house, so get out before it destroys you. Heaven is on earth and it should be in your heart. So if someone is stopping you from being in heaven, then get away from them.

❋ ❋ ❋

See Change

See Change is Ireland's national programme working to change minds about mental health problems. It works in partnership with over forty organisations to create a community-driven social movement to reduce the stigma and discrimination associated with mental health problems. The organisation is passionate about equality, and part of its mission is to ensure that everyone enjoys the same rights on an equal basis.

See Change wants to achieve an environment where people are more open and positive in their attitudes and behaviour towards mental health; where there is greater understanding and acceptance of people with mental health problems; where there is greater understanding and knowledge of mental health problems and of health services that provide support for mental health problems; and a reduction in the stigma associated with mental health problems and to challenge discrimination.

Some of its messages are the following:

- *Mental health problems can affect anyone at any time during their lives*
- *Mental health problems are part and parcel of being human*

- *People with mental health problems can and do recover*
- *People affected by mental health problems are entitled to the same human rights as everybody else in society without discrimination*
- *Everybody has the power to help stop the stigma and discrimination of mental health problems*

See Change: www.seechange.ie
Tel: (01) 8601620

⁂ ⁂ ⁂

belle

disappearing dad

Belle* is a tall, attractive woman, who looks strong and athletic. After she left school, she lacked direction and guidance and drifted into a bad relationship with Robert.

She soon became pregnant and they married and had three more children. Robert drank too much and took drugs and they had a stormy relationship.

Eventually Robert left Belle to bring up the children on her own with no support and no money. He had very little contact with the children and his parenting skills were dreadful.

Belle has had a very difficult time bringing up her children on her own. She feels that her problems were worse because she had so many children, so little support and she didn't get enough help from children's services.

I grew up in a nice ordinary background and went to a good school. My parents retired and moved to live in Spain just after I'd finished school, so I decided I wanted to get out of Limerick and have some fun. I headed off to London and worked in a clothes shop. Further education didn't appeal to me at the time – I didn't feel I could do it and, because I was young, I was more interested in having fun.

My parents were older and they were enjoying living

*Names, occupations, locations and other identifying details have been altered to protect identities abroad so they weren't very involved with me. I probably needed some guidance at that point in my life but I didn't get any.

In London I lived with a friend from Limerick and we had a great time. I loved the place. I was away from home and family problems, in this huge, exciting city.

I lost lots of weight while I was working in London and I looked really good. I didn't have much money for food but we went out every night. It was wild. We went to clubs and restaurants with different guys and were brought to lots of parties. We had a blast.

I came back to Limerick after a year because I felt I was getting burnt out. I had spent all the money I made working in clothes shops and restaurants because the rent in London was very expensive and I was going out all the time. I knew I wasn't progressing in life. I was sick of partying so I decided to try to get my life together at home.

When I came back, I stayed with my sister for a while but it was difficult because she was living with someone new and I was intruding on their relationship. She and her boyfriend were getting on with their lives and they didn't want to look after an eighteen-year-old.

Then I went to stay with my brother and got a job in a clothes shop in town. My brother's wife was expecting a baby and I felt I should leave and give them some space, so I went and got myself a little bedsit, which was awful. The back door and the window were broken and the shower was in what looked like a wardrobe. I opened up the wardrobe and there was a hose connected to the sink that you had to hold over your head and hope for the best. The oven was a gas ring that you'd use for camping and the place was so damp that when you walked on the carpet it squished.

I hated my job in the clothes shop because the managers were nasty and treated all the employees very badly. I was working just to pay the rent. In those days wages were very bad. Money was tight for everyone, flats were like slums and everything went on rent, so life was not very pleasant.

I had different boyfriends at that time and they were all from different backgrounds. I remember I went out with a motorbike courier who smelt of diesel, then a student who I adored, but he didn't adore me. I wanted to marry that guy because he was so funny, and when I got sick he looked after me like no one ever had. It broke my heart when a friend told me that he'd taken another girl to his college ball. She'd seen them lying on the grass together.

I was going out with a lovely guy called Michael when Robert came on the scene. Of all the people I went out with I was the most comfortable and happy with Michael. He was very funny and he made me laugh and feel good about myself. He got my sense of humour and I got his, and when we were together we did normal things like cooking and watching videos.

Robert owned a clothes shop near where I was working in town and I used to see him every day going in and out of his shop. We met in a bar near where we both worked and I thought he was exciting, attractive and good-looking. It's very hard for me to find anything good to say about him now, because I know so much more about him, but at the time I obviously found him very attractive.

In those days there weren't many places to go, and when I went out to the main nightclub in town with Michael we'd get quite drunk and I'd end up going off with Robert at the end of the night. I don't know why I did that to Michael because he was a lovely guy. I think I sabotaged the relationship because I didn't seem to have the ability to settle and be happy. I didn't feel like I deserved it.

I was very uncomfortable with Robert. I never felt OK about myself when I was with him. He was quite wild and he drank a lot. I drank a lot too, when I was with him. I think I was escaping from my life and myself by deciding to be with him. I was saying to myself, 'This is who I am now,' even though it wasn't. When we were together we were escaping together. We were in constant escape mode and I suppose I thought I was having fun. But deep down I wasn't happy with myself at all.

Michael got sick of me going off with Robert and he finished our relationship. I was broken-hearted but I hadn't been able to stop myself seeing Robert. Then Robert went off on a trip to America and I fell into another relationship with a nice guy.

When Robert came back I started to see him again. But it wasn't a proper relationship; it was like a series of one-night stands. If I saw him on a Friday night and went back to his place, I mightn't see him again for another week or two. I wasn't really going out with him. It was a series of chance meetings in bars and nightclubs.

I was only twenty when I got pregnant by Robert and I thought that when I told him that it would change our relationship. He was really shocked and very unhappy when I gave him the news. He was only twenty-three and he wasn't interested in being a father at all.

Robert had a terrible background. His mother had died when he was young and his father had been in prison for killing someone while he was drunk driving. Most of his family were alcoholics. He didn't have a good relationship with anyone in his family and there were always rows when they got together.

As soon as I told Robert I was pregnant he didn't want anything more to do with me. He stopped seeing me and went off with another girl. I was absolutely devastated and felt completely betrayed. I was so depressed that I wanted to kill myself, but I couldn't bring myself to do it. I think I was having a nervous breakdown. I sat in my bedroom and didn't leave the house, see anyone or take any calls for about two months. I was in a really bad state.

My parents came back to Ireland to celebrate their wedding anniversary and I pulled myself together to go to the party. I was determined not to let my family down, so I pulled myself together. I was about six months pregnant at the time but I was so skinny that no one noticed. I was wearing an amazing black dress and everyone said I looked lovely. It was the first time I'd been out of the house for months.

Robert came back into my life when I was eight months pregnant and said he was sorry and that he wanted to be part of it all. I naively thought that was great because I didn't want to be on my own. I got back with him and went to live with him at his sister's house. His sister was the only nice person in his family and she was very kind to me. The house was very rundown and had no central heating. It was in a very bad estate, so I felt isolated and lonely.

My parents said I could come and stay with them in Spain after I had my baby but they didn't want Robert there. Robert said that we all had to live together, otherwise our relationship wasn't going to work. So I stayed living with him and his sister until Madeline arrived.

The house was getting us both down after Madeline was born, so as soon as we could, we moved into the city centre. Robert's clothes shop was doing okay, so we had enough money to rent a modern house, but it was in a rough area. I was happy to be living on our own and loved looking after my new baby but I wanted to find somewhere better as soon as possible. I wanted to live in a better area near good schools so that Madeline would have nice friends and get a good education.

A year after Madeline was born we decided to get married. I'd been taking the pill but I'd been sick with a tummy bug so it wasn't working properly. I was shocked when I found out I was pregnant again and very upset that it was so soon. Robert told me that he'd look after me and everything would be OK.

We had a very small wedding. I was three months pregnant and it rained the whole day. I was miserable because I was suffering from morning sickness. Some of Robert's family were there but they didn't talk to anyone in my family and they drank their heads off and started arguing amongst themselves. I was really annoyed by their behaviour and eventually told them to leave.

I had a hard time with the second birth. Robert was drinking heavily and he arrived to the hospital drunk. I was in a crowded ward with only one bathroom and felt very unhappy and vulnerable. His family arrived at the hospital soon after Liam was born and they had all been drinking. They started to hold my new baby and were talking really loudly and I remember getting very upset.

We moved into our first decent house outside Limerick after Liam was born. We were only renting but I loved the area and was really happy there. I felt much more at home in the country than the city and I started to enjoy minding the two babies. There was a very small age gap so it was almost like having twins.

The shop was doing okay for a few years and we had another child, who was planned, and I was happy. We bought a small house and I was enjoying looking after the three children. Things seemed to be going OK until the business took a bit of a dip. Robert had started to drink a lot more and wasn't paying proper attention to the shop.

Our house was a wreck when we bought it. We tried to make it habitable but we didn't have enough money to do it up properly. We couldn't afford a new bathroom or kitchen but I did what I could to make it nice. I painted everything and sanded the floors. I made friends with the mothers in the area and the three children were in very good Montessori and primary schools. We could still pay for food and cover the mortgage, so I didn't worry too much at first.

I had started getting the bus into town, with the kids in a double buggy, to meet Robert when he finished work so I could stop him going to the pub. If I got to the shop before he left, he'd come straight home with me and drink at home. If he was out already it would be too late. I couldn't bring all the kids into the pub and drag him out.

Robert would drink anything. If he was at home it would be wine; in the pub he'd drink pints and spirits. He also smoked dope at home, which I couldn't stand. It was a real bone of contention between us because I hated him smoking dope in front of the children.

When the kids were young, that was probably the quietest time in our lives. Things got very difficult after that. The shop was being very badly managed and all the creditors started to close in on us. I knew that Robert was getting involved with criminals and moving stolen goods so he could make some money. When I found out what he was doing I freaked. Our finances were in bits and I was terrified the police would find out what he was up to.

Robert said to me, 'I can't do an honest job. I have to do something else to earn money.' The problem was that once he'd made easy money from criminal activity he wouldn't go back to working legitimately. It was too easy. There were these really dodgy guys calling to the house to see him and I used to tell them that he wasn't in because I wanted them to go away.

Soon I was pregnant again because I hadn't taken the pill at the right time. My life was in chaos. That was a very low time for me. I felt sick and depressed in every way. I had grown distant from Robert and he had from me as well. I started to realise that things had to change and I knew that I didn't want to be with him any more. I knew what kind of life I wanted and it didn't include him. He was staying out very late and getting more deeply involved in drugs. He was so drunk when he came home that he'd be messy and he often vomited on the stairs or wet the bed.

He behaved dreadfully in front of my friends and the parents who lived in the area. He started to really let it go. There was a mother in the area that I was very friendly with and she and her husband invited us out for a drink in the local pub. I don't know why I agreed to go. Her husband was a decent, respectable guy and he offered to buy Robert a pint. Robert said, 'I'll have a chaser,' and proceeded to get absolutely hammered.

We went back to their house after the pub and Robert started to use foul language. I knew they weren't impressed. They were civilised, cultured people. The whole thing was awful and terribly embarrassing. Then he lit up a joint in front of them and I wanted to kill him. The woman was very polite and flustered and was opening all the windows. She'd never experienced anything like it and didn't know what to do.

I kept hoping that things would change. I had three small kids, I was pregnant and I was hanging on desperately, waiting for Robert to get his act together. He promised me all kinds of things. He always had these grandiose ideas about how he was going to make it. At one point he was going to start a cutting-edge fashion label. Another time he was going to import Japanese clothing. I think it embarrassed him that he owned a shop and wasn't as creative or successful as he thought he should be. He wanted to be an artist but to me he was just a piss artist with delusions of grandeur.

I think Robert married me because I was from a good family, I spoke well and he thought I would make him look good. He had no education and his family was appalling. He had a huge chip on his shoulder about the fact that he was from a bad area. The whole lot of them were into any scam they could use to get money. They were always on the take and everything was done through the black economy. They were getting every kind of pension, disability benefit and cash they could, without declaring anything or paying any tax.

I remember calling my mother and telling her that I had

to leave Robert, that I couldn't bear another day of it. He'd started to get violent around that time and I was worried about the kids. He was violent in a weird way. He'd take out his anger on the furniture and the house but he didn't punch or smack me. I remember once he did take it out on me. He tried to strangle me when he came home drunk and I challenged him about his behaviour. It was very scary; I could feel my legs buckling underneath me.

There was a month or two of very tough times before Robert left. I had just had our fourth child and he didn't turn up for the birth. He kept staying out very late and when he came back he kept saying he was sorry. A month before he left, he came home with a diamond ring that he bought to replace my original engagement ring because it was a cheap one and all we could afford at the time.

What do you do when you have four children with a man like that? He had destroyed his business, wrecked the house and his presence was aggressive and damaging to us all. He had never bonded with any of the children because he was so wrapped up in himself and he gave them all a terrible time. He didn't know how to parent, so he would take out his frustration on them by being too strict and smacking them.

I have to admit that my children were driving me crazy. It was very hard work when they were small. But I did my best to be a positive person and I believed in doing the right thing. I was idealistic, hopeful and had standards for their behaviour. I used to make sure that they ate proper food and went for walks and I always did the best I could.

On the day Robert walked out, he said, 'See you later,' and he was gone. I didn't see him again for a long time after that. I was completely screwed financially. The only good thing that happened was that my father found out where he was and arranged for him to sign the house over to me.

After Robert left I felt very low. I thought I'd made a mess of everything and was a failure. He had completely shaken my confidence. He had gone off to live with another woman and even though he was a terrible husband and father, I was still really upset. The girl he was with was into drugs in a big way and I think they spent their time doing drugs together. I know that she left him when he ran out of whatever money he was spending on her.

I was very busy with my children after he left. They were all small, so I didn't have time to think too much about what had happened. People would call me and say, 'How are you? Are you okay?' and I'd say, 'I'll ring you back later. I'm busy cooking, cleaning, changing nappies.' I never got a chance to talk to anyone. I was so stressed that I lost a huge amount of weight. Ironically, everyone said that I looked really good and a bit of my confidence started to come back.

I had no money, so I had to go on single parents' allowance. I was barely able to survive and my family had to help me pay off the mortgage arrears we had run up. I was means tested for social welfare and when the guy came around to assess me I was embarrassed when he saw how I was living and what a state the house was in. I felt as if I was living on nothing. I had just enough money for food and had to go without lots of things. The gas and the electricity were regularly cut off and the house was damp and cold when we had no heating. I had to use an electric ring for cooking when there was no gas.

Robert didn't help at all, so it was incredibly difficult. He didn't even offer to buy the children a pair of shoes. I had to take him to court so that I could prove to the Department of Social Welfare that he wasn't able to pay me any money, before they would give me the lone parents' allowance. This really got me down. I thought it was wrong that he could get away with doing nothing. I didn't want to take money from the government and he should have been supporting his children.

Robert finally lost his shop and he had nowhere to live, so he went from bedsit to bedsit bumming off people and getting rent allowance. He spent some of the time sleeping rough and he was still doing drugs.

The kids were very difficult. They played up all the time and they were obviously acting out their pain. There was a lot of aggression and anger in the house and the eldest child was especially volatile. There was a lot of angst and moodiness and as soon as she hit her teens she discovered drink and dope and started doing them both. I think she was so hurt by her father's behaviour that she was self-medicating.

Robert used to regularly arrange to meet the children somewhere and not show up. It was always somewhere outdoors, like a park. I'd wait for hours with the kids and they'd all get really upset. It would have been better if he'd had no contact with them at all. I was overwhelmed by the responsibility and I badly needed a break.

I always took the kids on a holiday every year. Somehow or other I managed to get a cheap package holiday abroad. I thought it was important for them and for me to have a break. It used to break my heart when I saw other children playing on the beach with their fathers while I was there on my own with them.

For a long time I had no money and no partner, and the kids were giving me real trouble. I was so worried that I brought them to a child guidance clinic. The psychologist observed them playing in a room for a while. They played really well together, and she said they were fine and didn't need to go on any programme. I was naïve and lacked confidence, so when I was told that the kids were fine and didn't need any help I didn't argue with the psychologist.

At home they were attacking each other and were often uncontrollable. I didn't know how to cope and I'd end up losing my temper. I knew that wasn't the ideal way to manage them but I found them overwhelming. There were four of them and one of me. They could gang up on me and I couldn't physically control them. If they wanted to do something, I couldn't stop them.

They are all very bright and talented in different ways. They found things they liked in school and they're very sociable. What worries me is that they don't have a strong father figure and I'm concerned about the damage that has done to them.

Dating with four children is very difficult. When I met Chris I felt that he was a very caring, reliable and stable person. I liked dating him because he didn't have any unrealistic expectations of me. He was happy to call around to the house to see me and hang out with me. I didn't have to organise babysitters or get dressed up to go out.

Chris has always been quite detached from my children. He did the best he could with them but he wasn't crazy about them. I think it was hard for him because the kids were already so damaged by their father's behaviour. It was nice to have another adult around for some support and he has tried hard to help with them, but I think it was too late.

I found the children's services very unhelpful. When the children were younger I went to them and made an appointment for the two older children, who I felt had the worst behavioural problems. Initially we saw a registrar who was Indian. He was a fantastic psychiatrist and I felt he was making progress with them. Then he left and they were switched to a different, younger woman who was in her twenties. They didn't connect with her at all and she irritated them, so they refused to go back, which was very disappointing.

The schools were better. They spotted problems with the children's behaviour and dealt with it as best they could. They insisted on discipline but they couldn't force the children to study. One teacher asked me if it was OK if an educational psychologist assessed one of the children and I was open to that. I wanted to get help for them and the schools gave me good advice.

I think the best thing would have been if someone had come to the house and observed the children's behaviour with me over a period of time. I needed one person to get to know them and me and give us all support, advice and physical help. I was cracking up under the strain of trying to look after them and no one saw it. At one time I had to be taken to hospital with an ulcer. I felt let down by the health services and I was naïve about where I should go to look for help.

The two older children are much more affected than the younger ones. They have more memories about what used to happen when Robert was in the house and they missed him more when he left.

I think the kids were OK at the beginning of their teenage years. They all liked being in first year of secondary school but they all started getting in trouble during second and third year when they were exposed to drugs and alcohol. I think they were all looking to fill a gap in their troubled souls.

When Chris tries to correct them, they just say, 'You're not my father; you can't tell me what to do.' The youngest child has the best relationship with him. He's had no father figure, so he has bonded with Chris. The eldest boy has always tried to be the man of the house, so when Chris came along they were in competition for control and my attention. They pulled me apart; none of it has been easy.

Life is better having a partner but the children's problems are so ingrained that his presence hasn't made a huge impact. I'm more worried about the children now then I was when they were babies. I'm worried that they won't find their way in life and they will have problems with alcohol and addiction. My eldest child went through a really bad patch at sixteen. She was very depressed and volatile and spent all her time in her room, plugged into machines. I tried to get her to see a psychologist but she refused to go.

I blame Robert for their problems. He was a bad, bad influence on their lives. All through their childhood he'd pick them up and drop them. He tried to be their mate when they were older – the cool guy who would let them drink and smoke dope in front of him. He tried to make up for the past in the wrong way.

Individually they each recognise his failings but they now blame me completely for allowing him to be their father in the first place. They see him as such an inadequate individual that they say that our problems are 100 per cent my fault for letting him into my life.

I don't dwell on our problems a lot because I'd end up getting very depressed. I live from day to day and people who know me say that I'm very optimistic. I'm able to escape from the problems by keeping busy. I work, I read and go to the movies and theatre a lot. I do things that interest me.

I tried to work full-time over the years but I found that I was paying most of what I made to a childminder. I don't have great qualifications so I was never able to get a job that paid very well. I loved when I was working because I was able to get a break away from the children, which was beneficial for them and for me. But it was exhausting coming home at the end of the day and trying to cook dinner and get them to bed. It was too much to deal with them all wrestling and fighting with me. So it was probably slightly easier not to work. It's very hard to find part-time jobs. When the summer comes you have to give them up so you can look after the children full time.

I'm thinking about going back to college and I'm going to do that when the youngest has left school. It's fine for people to work when they have children if they have a good job and they're able to pay for a childminder. When you're on a low income your choices are limited and there's no such thing as a decent free crèche in this country.

I think Irish society puts everyone into a box. If you're not qualified for anything then you're working class and if you're from a middle class background and you've somehow slipped through the net, you're in limbo. You need help to get back.

I wasn't able to send the kids to the free crèches or free

after-school facilities because they wouldn't have fitted in. Things are very segregated in Limerick and my kids have a nice accent and went to the best schools I could send them to. I speak well because of my background, so I always felt that I couldn't fit in and people were wondering where I had gone wrong. People were either resentful of me because of my accent or looked down on me.

In England things are mixed up much more. Everyone uses free services because they believe they are entitled to them. In Ireland it's perceived as shameful.

My kids are bright and have great personalities when they are on their own. I think the pressure of us all being together with each other and having no money was too much. Their father had no input into their upbringing except in a negative way. I know they're going through a difficult time at the moment as they are in their teens, but I'm hoping they'll come through it and grow up to be happy, productive adults. They have good role models in me and Chris and that will help. I would hate for them to end up like their father.

⁂ ⁂ ⁂

Alcohol Action Ireland

Alcohol Action Ireland is the national charity for alcohol-related issues in Ireland. The organisation recognises that a huge amount of harm is generated by the way Irish people drink and the amount they drink. It has an impact on families, hospitals, workplace and policing – the economic and human costs are high.

AAI works to provide information on alcohol related issues and to create awareness of the potential harm of alcohol. It offers potential policy solutions for reducing the harm.

Alcohol is recognised as a potential trigger for domestic abuse in one third of the most severe domestic abuse cases. One in four admissions to hospital emergency departments are alcohol related and an estimated 61,000 children are affected by their parents' alcohol abuse.

AAI has made policy submissions on the dangers of the way alcohol is marketed to children at a very young age and the necessity of minimum pricing for alcohol so that it is not so cheaply and readily available.

Children are bombarded with positive images of alcohol and sixteen- and seventeen-year-olds spend an estimated €145 million on alcohol each year. People who begin to drink before the age of fifteen are four times more likely to develop alcohol dependence than those who start at age twenty or older. Suicide is a leading cause of death in young adults and alcohol use is a huge factor. One study of people who died as a result of suicide showed that half of them had alcohol in their blood.

People who are concerned by their drinking or the drinking of a friend or relative should contact their GP. There are a large number of governmental and non-governmental organisations in Ireland that will give help and advice to people with alcohol-related problems.

Alcohol Action Ireland: www.alcoholireland.ie
Tel: 01 8780610
Butler Court, 25 Great Strand Street, Dublin 1.

❋ ❋ ❋

jack

alienated parent

Jack[*] is a solid, direct, practical man with a caring attitude. He loves sport and is very focused on his career. He met Irina, who is Polish, while she was working as a waitress in a Cork restaurant. They moved in together and married quite soon after they met.

Irina missed Poland and couldn't settle in Ireland. She kept going back and forth between Ireland and Poland, and she continued to do this after their daughter, Angelika, was born. When the relationship ended she stopped Jack from seeing Angelika. Jack has tried to see his daughter over the years but finds it incredibly difficult to have a relationship with her because Irina has stood in their way.

It's very painful for Jack that he and his family don't have any contact with Angelika and he blames Irina for manipulating the situation and ruining his relationship with his daughter.

I grew up in a nice area of Cork. I was the eldest in my family and I had a good, happy childhood. There were no issues at home when I was growing up. My parents travelled for work so they sent me to a boarding school near Cork, which I liked. My other siblings were great. They all went on to third

[*] Names, occupations, locations and other identifying details have been altered to protect identities

level, did well, worked hard and are happily married.

I really took to school and enjoyed boarding. I think it was because I always participated in sports and loved rugby, athletics and tennis. My school was near the city so when my parents were back from their travels I could go home at weekends and hang out with my friends.

I didn't do brilliantly in my Leaving Cert – I was too busy playing sports and didn't knuckle down in time. I repeated my exams at a grind school and did better the second time. Ireland was in a recession when I left school in the 1980s, so I did a course in dental technology and decided to go straight to England and start work. At twenty-one I thought I was a man of the world.

Living in Birmingham was a rude awakening. It was tough to make a living and pay rent. I worked in a laboratory for two years and then applied for a job back home. I got a position as a trainee in a big laboratory in Cork and was very happy to come back. I stayed working for that company for five years and did further exams in clinical technology.

In my twenties I was in a rush to grow up and was very focused on my career. No one except myself was putting me under any pressure, but I was impatient and by the time I was twenty-two I felt I should be getting married and settling down. I think my attitude was due to the fact that I'd met a girl in Birmingham and the relationship had ended. She was the love of my life. I would have married her and I was very hurt when it was over. I wanted to be in a relationship again and I felt I had to make sure that the next relationship was committed and I was with someone who wouldn't run out on me. I didn't want to go through another break-up.

I met Irina in a pizza restaurant I used to go to with my

friends. She was Polish and was working as a waitress in the restaurant. Our relationship developed very quickly. Shortly after we started going out together she decided to pack in being a waitress and she moved into my flat to live with me. She was only nineteen and I was twenty-seven so I felt protective towards her and I was supporting her financially.

During the first year of our relationship I took a few trips to Warsaw with her and we met each other's families. We got engaged at the end of that year. I think one of the reasons I proposed so early was that the Italian guy who owned the restaurant where she had worked had his eye on her. He was competing with me for her attention and he put it up to me. He said that if I wasn't serious and didn't ask her to marry me then he was going to ask her.

When we got engaged I sat down with Irina's parents to ask permission. I was surprised that they said yes so easily. They were heartbroken that she was in Ireland but they didn't seem to mind the idea of her marrying an Irish man.

My family didn't take to Irina very well. They knew I was supporting her and living with her and were wondering why I was doing that. I didn't really mind. Irina was bright and spoke English very well. She was perfectly capable of working but she wasn't too keen on the idea. She just wanted to go out and socialise. I was working full time in those days but I didn't mind what she did – we were having fun.

We got married in Poland and I found the wedding traumatic. An Irish gang came over for the wedding and they were camping out in Poland for a few days and partying quite hard. Rows broke out between Irina and me. She was becoming quite controlling and was giving me ultimatums about how things were going to be done during the wedding.

She was a very demanding bride and was acting spoilt and wanted everything done her way.

The wedding day was difficult – there was some sort of big struggle going on in her family. I think they had only just realised she was going to live in Ireland permanently. There were also a lot of expectations and aspirations in relation to the kind lifestyle she was going to have with me.

I felt confused and under a lot of pressure. Most of the conversations that took place were in Polish and I couldn't understand anything. I don't think either of us was very happy about the wedding going ahead. If we hadn't been in Poland and everyone hadn't made so much effort to be there, I think I might have backed out. In the end we got married and went on our honeymoon and had a good time.

When we got back to Cork, we moved into a house I had bought near the same area where I'd grown up. It was never discussed but in my mind it was always understood that we were going to live in Ireland. My life was in Ireland and all my future earning potential was here. Going to live in Poland was not a runner for me. But Irina quickly made it clear that she was miserable in Ireland and said she wanted to go back and live in Poland.

I knew Irina missed her family and I got on quite well with her parents so I made a big effort to include them in our lives. We invited them over to Ireland a few times a year and she went back to Poland to stay at home for three months in the summer. She had made friends in Ireland but she kept saying that she missed the summer weather and the food in Poland. She never stopped saying how much she missed Poland all the way through our relationship. It began to grate a little.

I was sympathetic up to a point, but if I'm pushed too much I get angry. Irina knew how to push all my buttons. She tried to hurt me by telling me I didn't earn enough money, yet she wouldn't go out to work as a translator even though there were loads of opportunities available to her. She refused to commit to any job and was always anticipating the move back to Poland. I made it clear to her that it wasn't going to happen. There was so much uncertainty that I never got comfortable in the marriage. Before we got married our relationship was fun but after the wedding there was arguing all the time – it was always over the same thing: she didn't want to live in Cork. If we were in company it was embarrassing because she didn't mind arguing around our friends. There was quite a lot of sulking and freezing me out as well.

At one stage Irina took up a job in Poland for the summer. I didn't know what she was doing while she was over there and to me it looked as if she was never coming back. My family and friends thought it was an unequal relationship. I was keeping a home for her and holding the door open on our relationship while she ran around and did what she wanted.

Three years into our marriage her mother died suddenly and Irina rang me, very upset. I dropped everything for her and got on the plane to Warsaw and stayed with her for the funeral. She agreed to come back to Ireland with me and within six months she was pregnant. It wasn't planned and felt really out of the blue. She was very emotional.

The best period of our relationship was during the nine months of Irina's pregnancy. She was calmer and less volatile. She drank less and wasn't smoking and seemed really happy. She was doing all the right things. Angelika's birth went smoothly, but shortly after they came home from hospital Irina started complaining about Ireland again and said she wanted to go home.

Irina was maternal and I helped a lot. I did the changing and the night feeds and was enjoying the role of being a dad. I'd bought two houses and done them up just before Angelika was born. We were living in one and renting the other and I was mortgaged up to the hilt. It was 1999 so property was still affordable but it was a big mortgage and I was working hard to meet the repayments.

Irina didn't work while Angelika was young. She stayed at home and looked after her. When she was two she said she'd had enough of Ireland and wanted to move back to Poland. She was very emotional and spent a lot of time crying and had lots of long overwrought telephone conversations with her family. I couldn't understand it. We had a nice house, she had a lovely car and a good life. She was able to go to Poland whenever she wanted and had her family over to visit regularly.

Angelika was young so I allowed Irina to take her back to Poland. I needed a break from the situation and I thought if she went back for a while she'd get it out of her system. Some of my friends said that I shouldn't let her go but I didn't do anything legal as I was still able to see Angelika. I thought she would come back when she was ready to start school. But she got a job in Warsaw and I started to suspect that she would never come back. I was getting concerned that she might be having a relationship over there.

Eventually, I decided to get legal advice, and a friend put me in touch with a solicitor. The solicitor told me to wake up and smell the coffee. He said Irina was obviously gone for good and started talking about the Hague Convention on International Child Abduction, custody rights and things like that.

While Irina was away I had a brief fling over two months with another girl. I felt at the time that my relationship with Irina was over. The word got out and Irina found out. She came back to Ireland full of vengeance and said she wanted both our properties sold and she wanted half the proceeds. She said she could never live in our house again because another woman had been there. Irina put me under a lot of pressure so I didn't take a legal position on this. Property prices had gone up and there was equity in the houses, but I was finding it difficult to pay the mortgage. I wanted to start my own business and I needed some funds to do this, so I was tempted to sell. So without getting a legal separation, we sold the houses and the proceeds were divided. I rented an apartment and we put our money into separate accounts.

Despite all this, Irina said she was still prepared to work on our relationship. She didn't say she was leaving me or that she would never come back to Ireland, she just said she wanted the houses sold. She had a lump sum, so that gave her an opt-out clause if she wanted to leave Ireland again at a moment's notice. And that's exactly what happened a few months later.

—

I had no idea what was going on but I knew the relationship wasn't healthy. I couldn't explain the logic of what was happening to my family and friends, and I felt it was a huge price to pay for one liaison while Irina had been gone. She was full of venom and being around her was very unpleasant.

I still thought that if I agreed to let her go back to Poland again that she would bring Angelika back to Ireland for school, so I decided to let her go. Life with her was a misery but I made sure that the transition was orderly for Angelika. I was heartbroken for my daughter but we were still communicating. I knew where they were and that her being away was giving me a breather and time to set up my business. Irina went over to Poland, got a job and set herself up in a new apartment. I visited Angelika and stayed with them, so it was better than nothing. She would be handed over to me like a package for a holiday. I made lots of trips to see her when she was between the ages of two and five.

That all changed on one trip. Irina said she had decided that I couldn't see Angelika because of the affair. I suddenly realised what my solicitor was talking about. I was powerless and unable to see my child in a foreign country. I felt as if all the doors were closing. Fortunately, she didn't keep it up and the next time I went over she let me see Angelika again.

I didn't know what Irina's set-up was in Poland. I didn't know if she was seeing anyone but I suspected she was. While she was away I carried on a single life, as I was certain she was gone for good. Irina, however, still thought we were married and that I was bound by the rules of our marriage. I didn't think so but I kept communicating with her. We didn't have a formal separation agreement but I was helping her financially. She had her lump sum from the sale of the house and maintenance, so she didn't complain too much.

Irina suddenly decided to come back to Ireland just before Angelika was due to start school. I took her back, with some misgivings, mainly so we could be a family for Angelika again. She made a huge case for us staying together.

She said she was really sorry and manipulated me by playing the Angelika card and said it would be good for her if we stayed together.

We got back together but the damage had been done to the relationship. I think I agreed because I also still felt an emotional and physical connection to her. We had been together for a long time and there was an attachment there even though it was fraught with anguish. And I think I would have agreed to just about anything to get Angelika back to Ireland.

Angelika started junior school in Cork. Reality seemed to kick in and Irina was a bit more grateful to me for the efforts I'd made. A year of relative normality ensued but at Christmas, Easter, summer and any other possible time she'd be off to Poland.

I started to bond with my daughter and was really enjoying being with her. Things were still difficult but it was worth it because there were good times as well as bad times. Irina and I socialised together and we often had fun when we went out. Irina could still be quite volatile and wouldn't care if we had a row in public. I'd be mortified and would try to hide it.

When Angelika was seven, Irina filed for a separation. I was advised by my lawyer to stay living in the family home, which was a small apartment, because of Angelika. I tried to stay there as long as I could while we were going through the legal process. But it became impossible to stay under the same roof as Irina. She didn't want me there and asked me to leave by solicitor's letter, so I left.

Shortly after that Irina again asked if we could reconcile. Again, I tried to work on our relationship for a short while but it didn't last long. We were sleeping in separate bedrooms and she was very aggressive towards me. I knew I had to get out of the relationship. It was getting awful for Angelika. I didn't want her to witness us fighting and I'd had enough. Irina was trying to involve Angelika in the rows, giving out to me in front of her and she was getting too much information for her age.

Around that time I met Sarah and we started a relationship. She was going through a difficult separation as well and we got together quite quickly. It was towards the end of my relationship with Irina and she was living with her children in a house nearby. I moved out of the apartment I was sharing with Irina and into Sarah's place. It was early days but Sarah and I had a good bond and we were in a very supportive relationship. She's a totally different character from Irina, much more sympathetic.

I think there was a lot of damage done to my relationship with Angelika when I left. Sarah encouraged me to continue to see her but Irina was being very difficult. It would have been very easy for Angelika to feel that I'd moved away from her to live with Sarah. She met me with Sarah's children quite soon after I left and I'm sure she told her mother about them. I think that would have enraged Irina. She would have hated to think that I was trying to mix two families. There's no way she would have allowed that. Sarah and I realised that we had made a mistake by living so close and by allowing Angelika to meet Sarah and Sarah's children, so I was careful to keep them out of the picture after that.

While the separation proceedings were going on, orders were made for me to have access with Angelika at the weekends. That never happened. I never got overnight access and whenever I called in to pick her up, someone else would answer the door and say she wasn't there. I went to court to try to enforce the access but it was pointless. The orders were always being reviewed and changed but I still didn't get access. One judge actually said to me, 'Children vote with their feet.'

I went to court at least a dozen times over the course of the judicial separation proceedings. Each time I was in court I tried to describe the scenario to my barrister and got her to bring up the question of access. Irina would say to the judge, 'I'm not stopping access. He can see Angelika any time he wants, but Angelika doesn't want to see her father because he never shows up on time. He's never there; Angelika is always disappointed.'

The judge would note what she said and the order would continue but it was never complied with. Iriana's lawyers always said that I was late and didn't appear for access, which wasn't true. I even brought witnesses in to court to say that I did try to have access but that it was never allowed. The judges were very dismissive of my concerns. They would change around the orders and change the times of access, but my arguments were never taken into account. I had no voice in the proceedings. I had many conversations with my barrister but she always spoke for me to the judge. I never got into the witness box myself to give evidence and I think that might have been a mistake, but I don't know if speaking for myself would have made any real difference.

I felt that the courts were too focused on our finances. Irina's lawyers looked for major discovery in relation to the details of my business. The laboratory I had set up had done well for a number of years and I had already revealed my position to her. A lot of the money I'd made had been used to finance our lifestyle and much of it was gone by the time of our separation.

At one point I was given a week to take Angelika away on a family holiday. Angelika was eight at the time and she didn't want to go, but my lawyers told me to enforce the trip. Irina kept calling her on her mobile phone and telling her in Polish to call the police on her mobile phone. The gardaí did make contact with me and I explained the situation to them. Their advice was to bring her back to her mother.

But my solicitor insisted that I enforce the access so I locked the doors of the car and brought Angelika with me. She was fine about it afterwards and she accepted it. Irina hadn't given her any clothes or anything for the trip and it was obvious that Irina had no intention of letting it happen. I brought Angelika home after the trip and I never got her for overnight access again.

From then on Irina systematically withheld Angelika from me. Even if she was away she wouldn't let her stay with me. She wasn't allowed to come near me. If she hired an au pair she wouldn't let her answer the door to me and I'd end up speaking to her through the letterbox. I never knew when they were going to Poland and I ended up relying on others for information about my own daughter.

Just before the separation was finalised, a judge took Angelika into chambers and asked him if she wanted to see me. Angelika told the judge that she didn't want any contact with me. I couldn't believe it.

I think Irina stopped her seeing me purely for revenge when I finally left her. I think she lied to Angelika about me. It's called parental alienation. A parent who is alienating another parent will lie and go to any lengths to convince judges and psychologists that they are not the offending party. Irina did it when Angelika was three, four and five and then stopped for a while. Then she started again when she was eight. It's really sad because Angelika's cousins, grandparents, uncles and aunts haven't seen her for nine years, even though she lives nearby.

Despite what Angelika said to the judge, she did see me a few times last Christmas. She got in touch with me and we met up and had a few adventures in town and went out shopping. After that I sent Angelika a few texts from Sarah and me. That was a mistake. We got a really bad message back from Angelika that was obviously written by Irina.

During our relationship Irina was always able to criticise me without being specific. There would just be this tidal wave of criticism. She was able to bamboozle the judges in the same way. She would mix in absolute fabrications with a bit of truth so that it was very hard to argue with her. She is an arch-manipulator – no one would be able for her. She has huge strength of character and is able to hold a grudge like no one else. She's a very extreme person. I read a psychology book that perfectly described her personality type. She had this attitude that if she wasn't going to have me, no one else was.

When Angelika was eleven I made an application under Section 47 of the Family Law Act asking the court to look into what was going on. The court appointed a psychologist to do a report to find out what the problem was. We were all meant to meet the psychologist together. When we arrived Angelika was so wound up that she said she didn't want to be in the room with me. She wasn't brought in and she waited in another room. The psychologist said that we needed to have Angelika brought in on the meeting but she refused to engage. She didn't want to be put between her parents.

The psychologist didn't recommend making any more formal orders for access. He thought it was pointless. He asked for my agreement in relation to that and I went with it even though it broke my heart. He said that he wanted to meet with Irina and me so we could work on our problems.

At the sessions Irina covered up her efforts to alienate me from Angelika. The psychologist was in an awkward situation because something was obviously going on. He didn't know who was causing the problem. He wasn't going to tell us what he was thinking. But he did say that Angelika's trust was broken and that the only way to fix things was to deal with the deeper issues between Irina and me. He said that we would have to come together as parents and have open and honest communication and that unless we could resolve our issues there would be no chance for Angelika.

The psychologist put everything out there but he didn't give very specific advice. The gist of his report was that he wasn't recommending formal access. He wanted us all to continue to see him and to try to improve our relationships. He needed time to figure out if it was parental alienation or not. He verbally hinted at it but he couldn't say it outright.

I had done some research on parental alienation and I was certain that that was what was going on. Once or twice I stayed behind to talk to the psychologist and he more or less indicated that he agreed with me. In all those sessions Irina said that she tried to talk to me but that I always hung up the phone, was verbally abusive and was always hanging around her house. She tried to paint me as a monster parent on the loose.

Angelika got back in contact with me when she was twelve. She decided to see me on Saturday afternoons. I picked her up and went to her hockey matches with her and we had a normal father-daughter relationship for a while. She occasionally asked me for things like clothes and shoes but I wouldn't give in to all her demands. I think Irina was manipulating her behind the scenes and she was beginning to try to manipulate me too.

I met Angelika in school the odd time because she did after-school study, so she didn't get back home until late. She was always happy to see me when she had a break. If she texted me to come and see her I would immediately drop whatever work I had. I'd reschedule things to be able to be there when she was available. I thought if I didn't take up the opportunity she would have seen it as a rejection.

During second and third year of secondary school she was in and out of contact with me. Then she dug her heels in and wouldn't see me a lot of the time. I have no idea why she changed her mind. The head of the school was really good. I think she was traumatised by the situation, too. She tried really hard to help. She talked to Angelika and gave me lots of updates on how she was getting on and how she was.

Irina met a new man called Luan and went to live with him. Angelika was in transition year and all her work experience and trips abroad were arranged by Luan. I would find out by accident that she was working in places that I had connections with. Angelika would be near me but I didn't know where she was. I was always trying to track her down.

I spoke to Luan face to face on a number of occasions when I called to their house to try to see Angelika or to drop in pocket money for her. He came across as a reasonable guy. He said to me that he'd told Angelika, 'You've only got one father and you should try to see your dad.' I genuinely believed him. I don't know how Luan gets on with Angelika, but I think he's a good father figure and I know he brings her to hockey, drama classes and discos.

Irina and I settled our divorce two years ago. We didn't have a family home so there was just an order for maintenance, which was quite high. Things have been difficult for me with my business so I went back to court recently to look for a decrease in the amount. Irina represented herself at the maintenance hearing and she got so worked up that the judge told her to calm down. She tried to make out that I was living an incredibly extravagant lifestyle and that she was on the breadline. I know that's not true. She has since married Luan and he's well off.

The maintenance is for Angelika and I'm happy to pay it, but I would also like to be able to see her. Irina has told Luan that I do nothing for Angelika and won't provide for her. She's tried to damage my reputation. It's very hard for me to do anything for her when I'm not able to see her. She's never accused me of anything or told anyone that I've hit her or been cruel to her. No one has ever really asked her why she won't see me. She always said I was free to see Angelika any time and she didn't know why she wouldn't see me.

I've been going to another psychologist for the past two years. She's helped me to deal with the whole scenario. She started with a sceptical hat on and I know she was wondering if I was telling the truth. She wanted to know if I was genuinely interested in seeing Angelika. After two sessions she believed me.

She recognised that I had a problem and that the situation was having a big effect on me. She did a lot of work on that with me, using role playing and analysing my behaviour. She got me to change my behaviour. She said I should stop calling to their house and dropping pocket money for Angelika through the letterbox. She said I was rewarding their bad behaviour by doing that and that they would be looking out the window at me.

She told me to write to Angelika and she helped me draft a letter to her saying when I was available to see her. I wrote, 'Come out, have lunch, have a chat.' Then I would have to leave it up to her. She said I had to be careful about texting, phone calls and calling in because I could be accused of stalking.

The psychologist is convinced that Angelika will come back to me at some stage but I'm not sure when that will happen. She's helping me to deal with the situation emotionally and if I'm on a downer I'll call her. She says that Irina manages to continue the alienation without revealing what she is doing. Angelika is convinced that the battle is about money and Luan doesn't know what is going on. I don't think he's trying to alienate me but he's taking her side because I was giving them a lot of money and now it's less. That's why he came along to the court dates – it's all about finance. The fact that I'm not seeing Angelika is no big deal to him.

I've had no contact with Angelika now for over six months. Nothing. I get updates from her school and the school counsellor. I hear that she's a very polite, lovely, caring girl. She's doing well academically and she'll get into college, so I'm sure she'll do well in life. I don't know how she's doing emotionally.

I think about her every day and every night. It's like a bereavement I can't get over because the person is still alive. It's a desperate situation and I don't tell people about the sadness because it doesn't bear thinking about. I've said goodbye to her so many times. It wasn't fair on her – it was treating a child like a commodity. I do believe she will come back to me and I have to stay there for her mentally, physically, and financially.

My parents haven't seen Angelika for seven years. One day my mother bumped into her on the street and she was very polite but that was it. They feel a terrible loss and say prayers for her. They even went to the District Court to try to get access to Angelika. The judge said to them, 'If Angelika doesn't want to see her father then what chance is there that she'll want to see you?' and dismissed the application. They were made to feel small and insignificant. They gave up hope after that and felt that they had no rights. It's been a massive burden for me because my parents ask me regularly: 'How is she? Is there any news?' and I feel terrible if I haven't seen her. I end up saying, 'I've spoken to the school and she's fine.'

My psychologist said that I should forget about trying to help other people or make it OK for them. The main thing is that I keep having a relationship with my daughter. My sisters tried to keep up a relationship with her by sending her money and presents but they never got a card or a text back, so they eventually gave up. She obviously wasn't allowed, or she was afraid to make contact, otherwise she would have said thank you.

If you're in the situation I'm in I don't think there's

anything you can do about it. You don't know in advance if your partner is going to try to alienate you from your child or is going to use your child as a stick to beat you with. If I didn't want to see Angelika, Irina would have no power – the source of her power is the fact that I do want to see her. I'm taking a passive approach at the moment by not being confrontational about it. Irina is the type that never lets go and she'll never let go of Angelika until she walks out or someone dies. I don't know where her problem comes from.

No one here in Ireland recognises parental alienation as a syndrome. In the US they're starting to study it, but they're only learning about it. I wouldn't advise anyone about what they should do in this situation. You can't look out for it. It's not my job to educate people who ask me questions about parental alienation. I'm using all my energy trying to stay OK myself. No one has ever been able to give me good advice about what to do – not friends, lawyers, judges – no one. I realise that I have no control over this situation and that all I can do is control what is going on in my life, not what's going on in other people's.

❋ ❋ ❋

Parental Alienation Syndrome

Parental Alienation Syndrome *by Dr Richard Gardner is a controversial book that describes a disorder where a child is encouraged by one parent to belittle and denigrate the other parent. In situations of parental alienation (PA), a child expresses unreasonable dislike of one parent and becomes estranged from that parent. It is observed by lawyers and health care professionals as a dynamic in separating and divorcing families but is not recognised as a disorder by the medical and legal community.*

❋ ❋ ❋

kate

heaven is on earth

Kate* is a very witty, hardworking, determined person. She comes across as being both intelligent and impatient, with a rapid-fire delivery. She studied commerce in University College Dublin and thinks she suffered from depression in college. She dropped out in her final year and went to work in London.

Kate built a very successful career but allowed her life to be dominated by an on-and-off toxic relationship with Alan. She had two children with him and kept allowing him back into her life, against her better judgment.

When Kate discovered Alan was cheating on her again during her second pregnancy, she decided to separate from him. Even though they have an agreement in place, he has refused to support her and she has suffered severe financial difficulty because of his actions.

I was born in and grew up in Dublin. My parents were comfortably middle class, so we went to the ordinary local junior and senior schools. I was very bright in school and did well. I wanted to study law but that year the points were very high, so unfortunately I missed out by a point. I decided to do my next choice, which was commerce, instead.

I didn't have many boyfriends in school. I was very into

---

* Names, occupations, locations and other identifying details have been altered to protect identities.

activities and sports and I wasn't that interested in boys, I was probably intimidating to them. I'm quick-witted and opinionated. I have a very fierce intelligence and a really high IQ. I think this was a bit confusing for my parents because they were quite average and I used to get quite impatient with them. My father's family were more like me and I could see myself in some of my cousins, but not at home.

We got on well enough at home. My parents were quite conservative and a bit too strict. There was an attitude to alcohol. My father drank too much when he was in his twenties and thirties and he gave up drinking when I was nine. Consequently there was a fearful attitude to alcohol and I think both my parents had unresolved issues from the time when he was drinking. It was never really discussed, though.

I wasn't given enough freedom as a teenager. I wasn't allowed to go out late or sleep in on the weekends. I was the eldest and it was the first time my parents had dealt with a teenager, so they were making up the rules as they went along. I think my mother had this fear that we might end up in trouble or becoming alcoholics, so we weren't allowed to drink. She was quite fearful about us going out, and both my parents viewed socialising in pubs very negatively.

When I went to college I got on OK and I enjoyed the activities and social life for the first two years. My main problem was that I didn't really want to do commerce and was disappointed that I'd missed getting into law. I should have tried to change courses or repeat the Leaving Cert, but I felt under pressure because my parents had paid my college fees. I did fine in my exams at first, but then I had to repeat some of my third-year exams. It all got too much for me and I dropped out in my final year.

Looking back now I think I was suffering from depression. I don't think my parents understood what was happening. I knew something was wrong; I felt I couldn't cope, that I was struggling. For the first time in my life my appetite for competition wasn't there. I couldn't focus and I was failing exams. I couldn't put my finger on why it was happening. I gave up before my finals and walked out of college.

I felt terrible. It was hard to face my parents. I thought I was a complete failure, so I took off to England to get a job. Lots of students from my year were over in England working for multinationals, so I moved into a flat with some of the people I knew from my course.

I've always been brilliant at interviews and at selling myself. I come across as extremely bright when I'm talking to people so I do well at work. There were lots of Irish people doing well in London in the mid 1980s and lots of the people I knew from college did really well. They were working hard and making a pile of money. We were having a great time and we felt like fledgling Masters of the Universe.

Somehow I talked my way into a job as a stockbroker and threw myself into the work. I started to achieve again and was really enjoying myself. My first job was with a bunch of very clever, mad, eclectic people. A lot of them were Oxbridge educated and I loved their company, and they mine.

The really high achievers worked for the banks and consulting firms and had to be in their offices at seven in the morning and were expected to entertain clients in the evening, after a day's work. It was crazy. They became very wealthy CEOs and hedge fund managers but I think some of them lost a bit of their humanity along the way. I ended up working as a manager rather than as a broker because the hours suited me better. I did very well and eventually was promoted to director. I had friends who were earning megabucks but I was happy with what I was doing.

I had a few boyfriends along the way but nothing worth writing home about. Alan was my first serious boyfriend. He was a friend of a friend and we met in London. He was from Ireland and we were from completely different social and educational backgrounds. Alan's family was working class – his father had worked in a factory and his mother was a cleaner.

Alan had left school early and had not even completed his Leaving Certificate. He worked as a store manager in London. Even though he hadn't been to college he was very smart. He read a lot, and on the first night we met we discussed all the books we had both read and were quoting poetry to each other.

I was impressed by Alan. I thought he was an intelligent guy who hadn't had the opportunities I'd had. His family hadn't aspired to much for him so he had ended up in retail. He was doing well and making money because he worked hard but he wasn't doing as well as me.

We started seeing each other and for the first year it was perfect. We didn't move in together – he had his place and I had mine. He enjoyed my company. He liked that I was feisty and that I dressed well. My friends liked him because he was charming and intelligent. He was well able to keep up with our conversations. He was a handsome, attractive guy; he liked nice clothes and he always looked smart.

After a year I started to find out things about Alan that made me uneasy. He told me when we met that he wasn't in a relationship but I later found out that he had just come out of a long, serious relationship the month I met him. He had lived with a girl for a few years but he never told me about her. I would have been very reluctant to get involved with him if I'd known he was just out of a relationship.

I also wondered why Alan didn't call me sometimes when he was supposed to. I loved him but I felt that he wasn't as attentive as he should be, so I wasn't sure where the relationship was going. He told me a bit about his family and I discovered that his father didn't live with his mother a lot of the time. He seemed to have a weird arrangement where he would go off for months and then come back. It felt as if he had secrets from me and wasn't being entirely straight about himself.

During the second year of our relationship I was offered a very good job by the company I was working with in London. I would have to move to their office in New York. I told Alan that I was going to take the job. We weren't splitting up but I wasn't sure what was going to happen.

The week I was getting ready to fly out to America I discovered I was pregnant. I was on the pill but somehow it hadn't worked. I wonder sometimes did I have a subconscious desire to get pregnant. I was so sure I had taken the pill on time, but maybe I didn't.

When Alan came back to my flat after work that Friday, I told him I was pregnant. He told me categorically and unequivocally that he didn't want a child and he wasn't going to be there for me. He wouldn't discuss it any further and he said he was not going to get involved. I was completely stunned. I hadn't seen it coming. I was shocked by his callousness and coldness.

I went to New York and started working. I didn't tell anyone that I was pregnant. I was in shock and I was trying to think what I should do. A week later I had a miscarriage. In a way it was a relief because I don't know what would have happened if I hadn't.

I had a really tough few weeks. I was hormonal and there was nothing I could do and no one I could tell. I was supposed to be a nice middle-class girl, so telling my family I'd been pregnant was not an option. It would have gone down incredibly badly.

I stayed in New York for four years. During that time I came back to London periodically and I used to see Alan when I was there. He was good friends with my friends so we moved in the same social circles and when I met up with them he would be there.

The company moved me back to London after four years and I bought a nice house on my own as soon as I could. I'd been paid a bonus for the move so I was able to use that as a deposit.

Somehow or other Alan and I drifted back together and he told me that he loved me and he was sorry for what had happened while I was pregnant. He never explained the motivation behind his attitude. I was still in love with him so I let it go. He was living in his house and I was living in mine. He was reluctant to move in with me. I think he was seeing other women so that was probably his reason for not suggesting it. I think I also knew deep down that the relationship wasn't right, but I still never confronted him on the affairs that I believed he was having. He had the capacity to turn quite unpleasant if he was asked questions that he did not want to answer.

This went on for two years until I started to put pressure on him to make a commitment. He had opened his own shop and was employing a few people, so I thought, as he was doing well, he would be ready to settle down. At one stage I walked away and then I came back. I don't know why but I wasn't able to leave the relationship. I needed to know why he wouldn't commit.

One weekend Alan told me he was going home for his parents' wedding anniversary. I asked him if I was invited and he admitted to me that he had never told them about me. I had a work dinner on that week and I asked him to come with me. He said that he couldn't come because he was working. I was deeply disappointed. I felt as if the relationship was going nowhere. He then blithely admitted that he had been sleeping with a few people on and off and that this had started about six months after we first met. I was stunned and threw him out. I had a horrible feeling that I was the only one who didn't know.

When he came back from his parents' party I discovered I was pregnant again. I was careless that time. I think it happened because I was doing a lot of travelling for work and had got mixed up about time zones and forgotten to take the pill. I was getting up at 4 a.m. some mornings to get on a plane, so I was all over the place and wasn't thinking about contraception.

Alan absolutely freaked when I told him. He wouldn't talk to me and he disappeared. I said to myself, 'That's it! I'm going to have the baby and I will deal with it myself.' I told my family and they went ballistic; they totally flipped out.

They told me that I was bringing shame on the family. It was the 1990s, for God's sake!

My sister went nuts. I remember going home once during the pregnancy and she picked me up from the airport. She ranted at me all the way home, so I got out of the car and went to stay with a friend. My parents were so upset they wouldn't talk to me. I got no support from them. I felt terrible but I just decided I'd put my head down and get on with it. In my mind there are no such things as obstacles, just problems for which I haven't found the solutions yet. I'll get there but it may take a little longer with some things.

In the weeks before Michael was born I continued working and made plans for after the birth. I was in a very good hospital scheme in London. The midwife came to visit me at home, so I never had to go to hospital except for my scan. I'd sworn I wasn't going to join the baggy T-shirt and leggings brigade. I did go to antenatal classes and I met some very cool women there who have become very close friends. I was still the only working single pregnant woman in the place and it was quite a challenge for some of them to try to understand my obvious career success, my nice clothes, my well-educated tones and the Irish accent. It gave me a laugh most of the time!

I also felt strongly that I didn't want a child who didn't know his father and that if Alan wanted to be part of Michael's life, I would facilitate him. I discussed everything with him. I asked him what he wanted to do and he was fairly indifferent. He had no problem telling people he was having a child but he wasn't telling me what his involvement was going to be.

Alan crept back into my life for the final weeks of my

pregnancy. He said he wanted to be there for the birth. My sister was working in London but she wouldn't talk to me. I was the only one of my friends having a baby, so I felt very alone. I found that my friends weren't great at giving me any practical support, so I felt I needed Alan.

Michael was not OK when he was born. He had health problems from oxygen deprivation and I had to have an emergency caesarean. Alan was there at the birth and he freaked out and had to leave while I was having the section. Michael was a very sick baby and the nurses told me they thought he was dying. I was in a haze of drugs and painkillers when they told me.

Alan left the hospital even though there was a problem with Michael, and I was on my own with the news. He was happy to go off and drink pints to celebrate Michael's birth but he didn't want any of the responsibility.

Michael was in an incubator for a few days and then he was able to come home. I didn't know what the long-term implications for his health were going to be. I came home to Ireland with him when he was two weeks old. I was disappointed because my parents were very distant and embarrassed to have us in the house. They didn't want me to go out on the street in case the neighbours saw me. They hated that I was breastfeeding and I had to go up to my bedroom to do it.

Slowly Michael got better and he became a very bright kid. I had to go to hospital with him every month because the doctors were worried about cerebral palsy. Physically and emotionally it was a very tough year and I was quite traumatised. Four months after he was born, the nurses sent me photos of him they had taken while he was in the incubator. I cried and cried when I saw them. I think it was then that I realised he was OK and I could relax and love him.

I was struggling. I had no money from Alan and he refused to put his name on Michael's birth certificate. He saw his son occasionally, but my parents were disgusted with him and said that I should never allow him to see Michael. The job was going well, I just worked really hard and still advanced but it was very tough.

My mantra at that stage was: if anyone's going to fuck up the relationship between Michael and his father, it's not going to be me. I let Alan see him and I was trying to do the right thing. I wanted Michael to have a balanced relationship with his father. I felt I was being more than fair and that I was putting my child first. I was determined that I would take the higher moral position and never use my child as a bargaining chip.

When Michael was four, I got the opportunity to move back to Ireland. I was able to keep my job by working four days a week and travelling back and forth to London. I decided to sell my house in London and move back home. I thought I'd get more support in Ireland and that the education would be better. I saw people in England turning themselves inside out to educate their children. My neighbours' children were learning the violin at two and my friends were bringing their kids to interviews to get into top Montessori schools when they were three. The process of getting your child into a private school and the cost of education in England was a major factor in my decision to move back to Ireland. I saw how English middle-class parents behaved and I felt that they were ridiculous – they made such a big deal of everything. I thought that as an Irish single mother with a real job I wouldn't fit in.

I told Alan that I was moving home and he slapped me with a court application to stop me going to Ireland. He also applied for custody and access to Michael. He said in his application that he would be disadvantaged if his child was living in Ireland. He didn't want Michael but God forbid if anyone else thought that, so he had to be seen to fight for Michael. What other people think matters a great deal to Alan.

I went in on my own to the first court date and asked for an adjournment. It was extraordinary. The judge said to me that I couldn't leave the country until the application was heard. I said that I had to leave for work and that I left Michael with my family or minders in England or Ireland when I travel. The judge said I might abscond. I said to the judge, 'I have a job and if I wanted to abscond I wouldn't have told Alan about my plans to go to Ireland in the first place.' He saw my logic and didn't impose a travel ban on me.

I hired a solicitor and a barrister. As part of the process a social worker had to write a report. I was living in a decent area of London. The social worker came to my house and asked me where my parents were. I said that it was my house that I had bought and I lived on my own. You could see her shock and surprise – I didn't fit her pre-conceived notion of a single mother.

I brought a cross application for maintenance against Alan and I made him put his name on the birth certificate. We negotiated an agreement where I could move to Ireland but I had to bring Michael to London once a month and

Alan was supposed to come to Dublin once a month. I paid to take him over every month and it was expensive. Alan only turned up in Ireland once or twice. He paid a bit of the maintenance we agreed for the first year and he didn't bother after that.

I sold my house in London. There was a bit of equity in it so when I got back to Ireland I bought a house. I looked into chasing Alan for maintenance but trying to enforce an English order would have been expensive. It wasn't a huge amount of money and it would have cost a lot to pursue it.

If I were chasing a millionaire, then it would have been different. I didn't pursue it because it was a question of pride and being practical. If I started to rely on him for money then he would get right back in my head again and that was not going to happen. I knew he was unreliable and also a liar and that I would always have to take financial responsibility for Michael.

When I moved back to Ireland permanently my parents took to Michael wholeheartedly. They rewrote history in their heads and there was no acknowledgement of how they had treated me. I think their way of saying sorry and making it up to me was by being very good to both of us. They looked after Michael when I was away. They would drive him all over the place and I think they got real pleasure from being with him. He really bonded with them. Today they are without a doubt the best grandparents and parents anyone could ask for, they are truly amazing – even I can't hold a grudge for that many years.

Once or twice I tried to bring up the past but there was no point. It's just the fucked up way that Irish people relate to each other. I found it hard to forgive my sister; she had treated me appallingly and when she asked me to be the godmother to her child I said to her, 'Why don't you ask someone you actually like?'

Michael was in a good school, we had good friends and I was glad I'd come back to Ireland. I went into über-mum mode and got totally involved in the school board and became chairman of the committee. I made sure the meetings were organised for days when I was in Dublin. I also got involved in soccer coaching and the local church, and these activities grounded me. It can be lonely and isolating being a single parent and I recognised my tendency to get depressed. I created reasons to get up and get involved outside my home on the mornings I was in Dublin.

These were terribly important things for me to do. Work was often an unhealthy place to be. There was lots of drinking and late nights and I had usually been in the middle of the fun and frivolity, which is not always the best place to be. A lot of the people that I worked with or who worked for me were men. They had wives at home organising everything, so if we got out of a meeting early they'd be looking for the nearest bar. They had no impetus to go home. I'd be looking to get on the next flight back to Dublin to see Michael.

At that time Alan would flit in and out of our lives. He'd telephone Michael every night but their relationship lacked a real connection. While I was in London I bumped into him through our friends and we started seeing each other again. Michael was aged seven. I stupidly thought things were going to be better. I thought Alan had changed and now wanted the things I wanted.

My friends saw what I was doing but they didn't warn me not to get involved. I think that's because I have a strong personality and they were afraid to say anything to me. I really wanted another child and in some warped middle-class mentality I thought both my children should have the same father. After seeing each other for a year, Alan and I decided we would get married. It was agreed clearly and unequivocally that he was going to come back and live in Ireland with Michael and me and that I wanted to get pregnant ASAP as I was on the wrong side of forty already.

I paid for the wedding and it was small, simple and tasteful. There was no bridezilla crap! It took me two weeks to organise and I wore a lovely evening dress, not a stupid meringue. The service was by the local priest in the local church. It was intimate and everyone knew me. There was a lot of slagging going on in the speeches and I loved that. My friends were being witty and eloquent and I appreciated the humour. The tone of the evening was 'have a go at Kate'.

Alan got up to make his speech and he managed to talk for ten minutes without mentioning me at all. He talked about his son Michael at length and thanked all the guests, but that was it. I was stunned and mortified. I remember not being able to lift my head to look at my mother across the table from me. She had massive reservations and I couldn't bear to see her face that evening. Then we went on honeymoon and Alan refused to have sex with me. I remember being confused. I knew this behaviour was strange. I felt particularly unloved and unwanted right then. I was asking myself, 'What the hell have I done?'

I really wanted another child so I got pregnant very quickly after we were married. Alan was still in London but he was spending some weekends in Dublin. He was on the phone one evening, talking about work, when I asked him what was happening. He said, 'I'm opening two more stores in London; will you fuck off and leave me alone?' I was really annoyed because he had said that he was going to work in Ireland after we got married. I began to realise then that he was never going to come back – ever. I think he wanted a life like his father, where he could flit in and out of my life without really being there for me. That's the way it had been in his family. I rationalised his behaviour by saying to myself, 'He knows no different. It's behaviour he's learned from his family.'

I couldn't forgive Alan for not recognising his problem and not wanting to change. We all carry baggage but the child of an alcoholic can learn not to drink. You have free will; you can decide that you are not going to make the same mistakes as your parents.

While I was pregnant, Alan asked me to fix something on his email account. I looked through his mail and found out he was seeing two other women. I told my mother what I'd found out and she said to me, 'Well don't do anything while you're pregnant, because people will think you're nuts. They will think you're overemotional and won't take you seriously.'

I took my mother's advice and didn't tackle him on it. I knew from the past that when I cornered Alan about his affairs he was mentally abusive. He said that no one liked me, that I was a bitch and people talked about me behind my back. He said I'd driven him to have affairs with my overbearing attitude and that they had taken place before we got married, so they didn't count.

I was pregnant and highly emotional and under pressure. I was worried about how things were going to be financially because he wasn't helping me to pay the mortgage on the house and I was now pregnant and about to go onto statutory maternity pay of €100 per week.

We went to some counselling sessions in London and during the first session I cried my eyes out. Alan tried to say that he'd stopped seeing the women before we got married but that wasn't the point. He'd been seeing them at the same time that he'd been sleeping with me. He had obviously been lying the whole time.

At the second session I told the counsellor some of the nasty things Alan had said to me or that had happened, some even too painful to mention here, and she asked him, 'Why is it that you cannot care? Why are you so cold towards Kate?' He got up and walked out of the session. That was the end of the counselling.

I soldiered on through the pregnancy and tried not to be upset. But I wasn't coping. I kept working and I tried to switch off my feelings. Inside I was incandescent with rage but I didn't want to get upset because I felt that sobbing through my pregnancy would be bad for my baby and I had done enough of that with Michael.

Alan was still living in London. He never moved over to Ireland. He had no intention of ever moving. He bought more shops and spent more money on them and never sent a penny back to his family. Periodically he would turn up in Dublin. I said to myself, 'I'll do nothing for the moment; I'll keep a cool head.' My friends finally accepted that I wasn't ignoring what was happening. They knew I was holding things together until I had the baby.

In my head I accepted responsibility for my own actions. I had allowed my desire for another child to override my ability to weed the crap out of my life. I wasn't blaming myself. I just accepted that I had a degree of responsibility for what had happened. I had to do that if I was to find the courage to move on.

When Jane was born, the midwife said that they would have to take her to an incubator because she was having difficulty breathing. She tried to tell me she was fine but I started having flashbacks to Michael's birth and I got hysterical. I was paralysed from just having had a caesarean section and I went completely nuts. Alan left me to go home to Michael, and a few friends came in and helped me to calm down. Later that evening I walked up five flights of stairs to see Jane in the incubator.

The next day I got up and got dressed. I knew Jane was fine and I wanted to take her home. I was sitting on the edge of the bed when the doctor came to see me, washed and hair blow-dried, make-up on and dressing changed. He wasn't that surprised as he knew me well from the pregnancy. I think if I had similar surgery under different circumstances, or if I was a man, I would have stayed in bed for a week, but I had this visceral urge to take my child home, away from the hospital where there were bad memories.

Alan left me two weeks after Jane was born. That was it – he was gone. I remember my birthday when Jane was four weeks old. I was on my own with my new baby and no husband. I had some money but I had to resign from my job as I knew it was too much to ask my parents to look after Jane as well as Michael, and it had all got too much for me. I couldn't keep doing the job and the travelling with two children.

I fell into a deep depression, which was hardly surprising. I should have been hospitalised and medicated, because I was beyond grief. I spoke to my GP about it and I said, 'I can't go to hospital because I can't let the balance of power change between Alan and me. He would use that against me.' The GP was great. She supported me and because she knew how strong I was she didn't classify me as completely barking mad.

When I tried to talk to Alan at that time, he said to me, 'I hope you get cancer and die, you cunt,' at the end of every conversation. He got more and more vicious. He was totally irrational and accused me of not understanding him and holding him back. My parents tried to talk to him at one stage and said to him, 'Do you not understand the woman you have married? She won't put up with this behaviour.'

Eventually, I got focused about what I had to do to end the marriage. When Jane was one I went to see a solicitor so I could get a separation. I didn't agree with the idea of trying to negotiate from zero, so I wrote out what I wanted in a draft agreement and gave it to the solicitor. I thought it would be better to argue about tangible issues, as Alan was incapable of forming a coherent thought by that time.

Alan wasn't easy to deal with. I found out that he owned stuff that he hadn't told me about. I said I would take him to court if he didn't agree to a separation. He agreed to sign up to all sorts of things: the house was signed into my name and he was going to pay our health insurance, school fees and maintenance. The amounts weren't huge or unrealistic, but to date he hasn't paid a penny. My solicitor looked for his fees and I said, 'If you can give me an agreement I can enforce, I'll pay your fees.'

I can go to court and have an order made on that agreement. Then I can have the order executed in England.

If Alan fails to comply with the order I can have him arrested in Ireland. The thing is that it would cost a lot of money and it probably wouldn't be worth it. I have to think about who would benefit and who would suffer if I put Alan in jail. I'm not prepared to go that far and have to explain why Daddy's in jail to my kids. I've spent five years trying to get him out of my head and I'm not going to let him back in by engaging with him. I have to put my sanity first, my children second and the money last. Money isn't everything. Anyway, Alan is clearly unwell and in need of help, you can't rationalise with irrational people, so why even start?

I survived on welfare for four years, and in the last two years I've been working on lots of different types of consultancy jobs. I had four years of nothing. I couldn't live on social welfare. I got into huge arrears with my mortgage – over €100,000. In the last six years I've had two sets of proceedings brought against me by my bank, looking for the repossession of our home. I have managed by using every bit of my intelligence and wit to talk my way out of both sets of proceedings.

I am nothing if not determined. I went to lots of meetings with my bank manager and said to him, 'Don't judge me by what you see now. This is a blip in my career path. I have made lots of money in the past and I will again. Do not put me on the street, because by God I'll make you pay for it. It's a twenty-five year mortgage and you need to be pragmatic. You have to amortise it over a longer period.' I think I was so angry I was certifiable.

I always engaged with the bank and because of that they were prepared to listen to me. I said to them, 'There is a job out there for me. My children haven't seen their father for a year.' I appealed to their humanity. I think the only reason my house was not repossessed was because of my powers of persuasion and because I never, ever give up.

Before one meeting with the bank the stress really got to me. I went to see my GP and I ended up sobbing hysterically on the floor. I told her I couldn't live like this. I was so stressed. Stress is a killer and it's hard for people to understand what it's like to be left destitute. At one point I went for a month without heating or a phone. I did not sleep properly for over three years and was admitted to A&E twice with chest pains due to stress.

At one stage the bank was looking at my expenditure and they said that I was paying too much for school fees. I get a grant from the school and everything else I had went on fees and the mortgage. I said to the bank, 'The fees are a long-term investment in my child's future. They're off the table. I will never, ever discuss this with you again. I have told my children, "Your only job is to do well in school and justify the effort I have put in. Let me worry about everything else."'

All the proceedings for repossession have now been struck out and I've got a new job starting in a few weeks with a decent salary. The only thing that's kept me going is that I have massive, deep reserves of strength. I dig deeper into myself than anyone I know. I've never rolled over and given up. When it comes down to things that are really important, I am strong and pigheaded.

Some friendships have suffered along the way. I wasn't a nice person to be around for about two years. The stress, worry, panic and fear that everything will fall down if you do not remain focussed can leave you with little time for the niceties of friendships. Those losses I do regret. Other friendships failed because back then, while everyone was feasting off the Celtic Tiger, being poor was like having cancer – people crossed the street in case it was catching.

When things were bad, my faith was very important to me. My children aren't sick and it is only money. Every so often I repeat that to myself: 'It's only money.' I have to bring it down to that; I have to have perspective or I'd go mad.

I have a barter system for lots of things. I'm a good cook so I make food for people and they do things for me. I can be very resourceful. The definitions of value and worth have changed for me. I don't assess things in monetary terms any more as it is really about what they are worth to me right then. Offering some help with French homework and getting babysitting in return can be a fair deal – it's not about hourly rates.

Jane is getting older and she hasn't seen much of her dad. She idolises him but she doesn't know him. She's a lot like me: she's funny, feisty and a very strategic thinker, and she's had an amazing ability to both charm and mess with people's heads from the day she was born. She says the most astonishingly perceptive things. She waits for her dad sometimes when she thinks he's coming. She'll sit there for hours at the door. I know that if she's disappointed too many times that she'll go crazy. She will not take that easily from Alan. She will reach a stage some day where she'll have a kick down fight with her father and say to him, 'What the fuck have you been doing for the past twenty years?' I think Alan is living in a fantasy world when it comes to his relationship with the children, because the children have been so accommodating. I have made them send birthday cards, Christmas presents and photos to their father even though there's often nothing in return.

Michael is a beautiful, spiritual, thoughtful child. He might become a doctor, as he seems to have a true vocation for caring. He has a way about him. He's so smart he could be anything he wants to be. I know our situation hurts him every day. The only thing I can do is to try to help him expel all the emotions he keeps bottled up inside himself. I push him to express himself every so often. Sometimes I rant and rage and Michael says to me, 'You cannot expect me to fight with my father.' I think that's an extraordinarily perceptive thing for a child to say.

When Michael was ten, Alan didn't see the children or call them for a whole year. Michael couldn't cope with it. He thought Alan was lying dead in a gutter somewhere. Even Alan's mother didn't know where he was. Then Alan got in touch and asked them to come over to London. Michael was thinking of going over but for the first time I decided I wouldn't let him. I thought it wasn't right that he be allowed to pick him up and drop him when he felt like it. I don't want him to look back as an adult and think that he rolled over whenever his father wanted to see him. I wanted to protect him from an abusive relationship and to have a strong sense of self-respect. I don't want him to end up in an emotional turmoil when he's in his twenties. I think things have got to a point now where Michael is very disappointed and the lack of love is tangible.

I've made appointments for Michael with child psychologists and counsellors over the years and he's far more receptive to it now as he has gained clarity over the situation. I think it's important for him to have someone to talk to who does not have a vested interest in the outcome.

I thank God every day that his school has such a strong pastoral care programme, and the staff have been wonderful with him.

I've made a conscious effort to provide strong male role models in my children's lives. I have very good male friends from my own childhood who have rocked up and taken them under their wing. I know that my children trust these guys and my other close friends and that they can talk to them.

I am lonely now. I've no partner but I'm not entirely unhappy about that. There was no way I was going to parade a load of men through my house over the years. I made a decision to have my children with Alan and I will live with the consequences. I think I will get there eventually and have a relationship some time in the future. I meet a lot of great, nice people and I have a lot going on in my life, so something will happen.

I think that there was some deep reason why I was attracted to Alan. I don't know what it was but it might have something to do with my restricted upbringing and the attitudes in my home. There was definitely some sort of co-dependency thing going on.

I've learned a lot about myself. I'm not going to apologise to anyone for being bright and I'm a great friend. Everyone knows that they can call me if they're in trouble and I'll come without question. I'm the one you want in a crisis.

However pissed off I get, however aggrieved I am about my life, I always look at my kids and I know that I'm doing OK. They say you get your reward in heaven but I think you get it by watching your kids grow up into fully rounded members of society. I do hope they'll appreciate everything I've done for them. Maybe when they're grown up, happy and contented, maybe rich, maybe famous, (hopefully both) and when someone asks them how they got there, they'll simply say, 'My Mum.'

❋ ❋ ❋

MABS

MABS (Money Advice and Budgeting Service) is a national, free, confidential and independent service that provides advice and support to people in debt or in danger of getting into debt. Each MABS company is located in the community it serves and works to help its clients with debt management, budgeting and developing good money management skills.

The organisation recognises that more and more people are experiencing problems with money, budgeting and mortgage arrears and that financial difficulties can affect everyone from high-income earners to people on a low income.

If you are dealing with financial problems, the organisation gives the following advice:

- *Don't ignore the problem: the longer you leave it the worse it gets*
- *Don't borrow more money to pay off your debts without getting independent advice*
- *Contact everyone you owe money to ask them to give you more time to repay your debts*
- *Check your rights and entitlements with the Irish Financial Services Regulatory Authority*
- *Be open and honest with your creditors*
- *Always attend court hearings and take a copy of your personal budget*
- *Keep copies of all letters you send and receive*

MABS: www.mabs.ie
Helpline: 1890 283438 (Monday-Friday 9 a.m. to 8 p.m.)

❋ ❋ ❋